15.99

741

Creating

creature comforts ™

Creating

creature comforts™

Andy Lane

BOXTREE

contents

First published 2003 by Boxtree
an imprint of Pan Macmillan Ltd
Pan Macmillan, 20 New Wharf Road, London N1 9RR
Basingstoke and Oxford
Associated companies throughout the world
www.panmacmillan.com

ISBN 0 7522 15647

Produced under license by Aardman Animations
© and TM Aardman/Creature Comforts

Text © Aardman Animations Ltd

All rights reserved. No part of this publication may be
reproduced, stored in or introduced into a retrieval system, or
transmitted, in any form, or by any means (electronic, mechanical,
photocopying, recording or otherwise) without the prior written
permission of the publisher. Any person who does any unauthorized
act in relation to this publication may be liable to criminal
prosecution and civil claims for damages.

9 8 7 6 5 4 3 2 1

A CIP catalogue record for this book is available from
the British Library.

Design by Dan Newman, Perfect Bound
Printed by Butler & Tanner

foreword

by Nick Park

Clay animation, until 1979, could be summed up in one word – Morph! Peter Lord and David Sproxton created the loveable, cheeky plasticine character for BBC Television's *Hart Beat* – a squeaky sidekick for artist/presenter Tony Hart. Squashing, stretching and metamorphosing, the malleable Morph typified all that Plasticine could offer as a medium for animation, or so it seemed.

I recall, toward the end of my Communication Arts degree at Sheffield Polytechnic, a tutor asking if I'd seen the new *Animated Conversations* series on BBC 2. He praised the innovative way the animators had taken 'fly on the wall' voice recordings of real life conversations of ordinary people, then created characters and animated their mouths and body gestures to fit these voices. The results were enthralling and the series was the talk of the Art Faculty, but I remember how my Dad enthused particularly about 'the Plasticine one – in the Salvation Army Hostel' and was struck by its 'pathos and acutely observed human mannerisms'. The film in question, *Down and Out*, was also from the creators of Morph. Not only did its sophisticated style set a new bench mark for plasticine animation, but the film itself was a milestone in its technique.

The sound track for *Down and Out* was a recording of a 'real moment' in the life of a homeless man attempting, unsuccessfully, to get a meal in a hostel. The characters were clay models caricatured but still very 'human', sometimes moving with subtle nuance, then perhaps with a deadpan expression. The result was very funny but tragic and profound at the same time giving it a level of pathos rarely seen.

Following *Down and Out* came *Foyer Girl* and then the series *Conversation Pieces*, this time for Channel 4. Although the idea of animating characters to match 'real' recorded conversations wasn't original, the technique was quickly becoming Aardman's signature.

This took Aardman into the late 1980s and *Creature Comforts*. Channel 4 commissioned the company to make a series of five short films under the banner of *Lip Sync*. Pete and Dave asked me to make one of the films and whilst I was interested in animating natural conversations, I decided to put the words into the mouths of animals. After interviewing people of various ages and nationalities, asking them to describe the way they lived, what they liked and disliked, about food and the weather, when I listened back to the tapes I realized the answers could come from inmates in a zoo.

Since making the original film I have often wondered what animals might have to say if asked about other subjects, gardening for instance, or a day out at the seaside, or even how they evolved. I felt as though there was a whole world outside of the zoo that creatures would have interesting and amusing views on. As I was busy on Wallace and Gromit, I asked my long-time colleague, Richard Goleszowski if he would like to take on the project. I felt that Golly, as he is affectionately known, could take my basic ideas and develop them into new and perhaps quirkier areas. I'm delighted to say that he has certainly achieved this.

I would much rather you saw the finished films than try to impress you with the technicalities of how they were made, but this book is an opportunity to go behind the scenes and appreciate many unsung talents; it illustrates the expertise of all those involved behind the camera and microphone.

Well done to all the team, and I hope you enjoy this book.

Nick Park

foreword

by Clement the Bloodhound

Clement reflects
on the making of
this book.

People often say to me, 'Clement, old son, you've had so many experiences with doctors and hospitals and suchlike over the years, you should write your life story.' I tell them I would've tried years ago, but I get cramp in my wrist whenever I hold a pen for more than a few minutes. So they say I should use a computer, but I tell them I don't have any truck with computers. Not my cup of tea.

Actually I did try to get a few publishers interested in my life story some time back, but most of them told me to sling my hook. Quite dispiriting, I found it. Quite dispiriting.

Anyway, I've been asked to say a few words in the front of this book instead. It's the story about the making of the new *Creature Comforts* TV series, which I took part in. A very charming young lady came round and talked to me for hours about my views on the National Health Service. Well, I've seen so much of it over the years. Seen it from the inside out, you might say - which is what quite a few surgeons could say about me, I expect.

Now, I have to be honest, I've tried to read this book but my eyes really aren't up to all this print. I've had them looked at, but I don't like the way the doctors clamp your head in some kind of big... clamp... and bounce things off your eyeballs. I'm no expert, but I would have thought that that does more harm than good. Anyhow, this book is much too heavy for me to hold for any length of time, what with my wrist and all. But I am told by those-in-the-know that this book contains a great deal of entertaining material and behind-the-scenes stories about the making of *Creature Comforts*.

There's lots of photographs of me in it, I understand, and a few photographs of the other animals that were interviewed for the series. Between us we cover quite a bit of ground, talking about all kinds of things from gardening to Christmas. There's even a bit about food – I know that because the girl who was doin' the interviews asked me about my favourite food, and I told her… I told her that I liked pheasant. Nothing like some pheasant, I told her.

Sorry, what was the question again?

"Sorry, what was the question again?"

"I'm loyal to the point of disloyalty."

introduction

Big budget Hollywood movies are now filled to overflowing with mythological, prehistoric and alien creatures. The odds are they have been created using computer-generated imagery, also called CGI. The costs are astronomical, the results incredible, and the limitless possibilities the technology affords has led to its increasing use.

But in an industrial park near Bristol, at Aardman Animations, a group of dedicated men and women are sculpting small creatures with outsize mouths using Plasticine. They are using it to make short, quirky and endearingly personal films, and they are doing it at the rate of about four seconds a day.

Mocked-up poster artwork for the waiting room at the vet's surgery.

The technique they use is called stop-motion animation, or sometimes claymation, something of a dinosaur itself in today's high-tech world where computers can create absolutely anything. Stop-motion animation means that the animators take a series of photographs of their little models. To make one walk they must stand it in position, take a photo, then move the left leg a fraction, take another photo, move it another fraction, take another photo, and so on. When the photos are projected in rapid succession on screen, the model is percieved to be actually moving. To get just one minute of film they have to repeat the process almost fifteen hundred times. It's labour-intensive and time consuming, yet can still be a great success.

Although stop-motion animation has been used for nearly a century, its revival has a lot to do with a short film entitled *Creature Comforts,* first shown in 1989. It was made for Channel 4 by Aardman Animations and was directed by Nick Park. Neither were well-known to the public when *Creature Comforts* appeared, but both are now big names. Nick still directs films about talking animals made of Plasticine, but the films now last a lot longer than five minutes and they can – and do – compete with Hollywood at its best.

The great thing about *Creature Comforts* was that it was a programme that appealed equally to kids and adults. It had the attraction of a puppet show injected with human banality and ordinariness that set it apart from everything else. There's a jaguar draped lazily over a branch, complaining about double glazing, an enthusiastic terrapin with big teeth and large spectacles, and a family of polar bears who just can't stop interrupting each other. These are hardly the

"The chicken was so horrible, I could vomit all night and never stop"
Babs the pigeon

stuff of which TV legends are made and yet, nearly fifteen years after these talkative creatures first appeared on our screens, we remember them with affection. It's as if they were our neighbours.

A lot has happened since then. The world is a different place, TV programmes are now much slicker, thousands of films have washed over us in the cinema and from high-tech home entertainment systems, and yet there's still a little part of our minds and hearts that are forever made of Plasticine.

Before *Creature Comforts* was screened in 1989, Aardman Animations had already produced a series of popular inserts, for the BBC's *Take Hart* (1978-1984) programme, starring an animated character called

More posters and magazine covers used to dress the vet's waiting room.

Morph. Aardman had also made a number of serious pieces for Channel 4 in which pre-recorded conversations were painstakingly placed in the mouths of realistic Plasticine figures. These films fell more into the category of art than entertainment. The arrival of Nick Park, an animator who came straight from the National Film and Television School in Beaconsfield, brought a distinctly exaggerated style that sent Aardman in a new direction.

"The more sort of, intrusive the dentistry, the better I like it really."
Mazulu & Toto

A slug is for life...

...not just for **Christmas.**

As with Aardman's previous films, *Creature Comforts* used real interviews with real people, but the way Nick animated them contrasted with what was being said. The result was bizarre, instantly watchable and curiously addictive. The first time you watched it the talking creatures were the highlight, but thereafter one spotted the funny and sometimes bizarre happenings in the background.

No-one could have envisaged what would happen when Nick Park arrived at Aardman. He not only directed *Creature Comforts* but brought with him a partially completed, animated short film featuring an eccentric inventor with a taste for cheese and his sensible dog going on a trip to the moon. Aardman helped him finish the film, and it was shown on the BBC in 1989 as *A Grand Day Out*. The two principal characters, Wallace and Gromit, have since become known worldwide, and their adventures continued in two more short films, *The Wrong Trousers* (1993) and *A Close Shave* (1995), and in a series of short sketches with the overall title *Cracking Contraptions* (2002).

HOME CASTRATION

YOU KNOW IT MAKES SENSE

The popularity of Wallace and Gromit created a demand for merchandise, and it was soon possible to buy a range of products from cufflinks to car mats. Aardman's unique animation style also led to commissions for hundreds of adverts, and its characters have sold everything from American Express credit cards to Weetos. The success of the *Creature Comforts* short film led to the creation of a much-loved advertising campaign for Heat Electric using some of the characters from the original film.

If the Heat Electric campaign defined Aardman in the minds of the public, and Wallace and Gromit are its best-known characters, then Aardman's pop video for Peter Gabriel's single *Sledgehammer* (1986) is the studio's creation that gets the most airplay. A pop video incorporating stop-motion animation is something of a rarity, if only because of the sheer amount of time it takes to produce, but former 'Genesis' front-man Peter Gabriel often commissions contemporary artists to produce work for his record covers. The *Sledgehammer* video frequently gets voted close to the top of the best pop videos of all time, and it's a great showcase for Aardman's achievements.

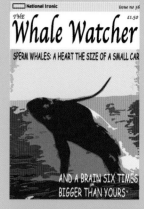

Over the last fifteen years, Aardman has continued its serious and funny animation, while making commercials, pop videos and full-length cinema films. Directors at Aardman Animations have also won several Academy Awards™ and BAFTAs, and been nominated for many more. In 2000 *Chicken Run* was released, a full-length movie, with the voices of

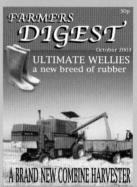

Mel Gibson, Julia Sawalha and Miranda Richardson. It told the story of a group of chickens whose fate was inextricably linked with flaky pastry and gravy until the group decided to mount an escape from its Stalag Luft-like coop. The film was financed by DreamWorks SKG – the Hollywood company set up by David Geffen, Steven Spielberg and Jeffrey Katzenberg – which meant, ironically, that the people helping to develop cinema's newest animation technique, CGI, were contributing to the survival of one of its oldest.

Aardman's latest project is a second series of *Creature Comforts* using the same stop-motion animation technique, the same style, some of the same team and a few of the original interviewees from the Heat Electric adverts.

This book is going to delve right back into the Aardman archives to look at the genesis of the original *Creature Comforts*. It will also provide some details of the new version, taking you through the process of making the episodes from the commissioning stage to the final edit and music scoring. It'll also let you into some of the trade secrets.

In a world where CGI is the norm, where alien creatures and fantastic monsters can be generated almost at the press of a button, it's reassuring to know that there's still a cottage industry based in Bristol that's selling its products all over the world. And it's even nicer to know that the product in question is a result not of technology but of craftsmanship and artistry.

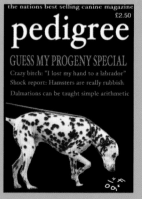

Part One:
First Things First

what is stop-motion animation?

Just as every little boy wants to be a train driver, every adult man wants to be a film director (at least those who don't want to be a film star, rock star or footballer). The problem is that you just can't start making a film and expect to be any good – it requires training, knowledge and experience. And it's hard to get that experience because you need cameras, lights, sets, actors, scripts... not the kind of thing you can rustle up on a rainy Sunday afternoon.

But what if you set your sights a little differently? What if you direct animated films instead of live action ones? Sure, you still need the camera but everything else is negotiable. At a minimum, all you really need is a white surface, a pen and you're off, limited only by your imagination.

Right: The Aardman creature workshop, where the models are constructed.
Bottom: Fluffy the hamster was previously called Gumbles.
Opposite: Megan and Gladys are prepared for their big moment.

Most of the people who work in animation started when they were young. Once you understand the basic theory, it's simple. Animation – like live action filming – depends on the fact that if the eye is presented with a sequence of still pictures at a fast rate, it will blur them together and create a moving image. And that's what a film is: individual pictures projected onto a screen, at the rate of twenty-four per second.

With live action films, the pictures are taken in real time. If James Bond spends ten seconds walking down a corridor in the evil villain's HQ, that's because the actor playing him took ten seconds to do it on a film set. The camera takes a picture of the actor every twenty-fourth of a second, one after the other, after the

16

other, dividing one continuous action into separate slices. Consequently, that ten-second walk actually consists of two hundred and forty separate, still photographs. But in animation the pictures don't have to be taken in real time. If a model car is being photographed moving across a table top, it doesn't matter whether there's a few seconds between each picture or a few hours because the result would look exactly the same.

Animation can be divided into two types, the 2-dimensional type and the 3-dimensional type. The 2-dimensional is practised by Walt Disney and does not concern us here. The 3-dimensional is the one practised by Nick Park and Aardman Animations, and it's worth spending a little time investigating how it's done.

3-dimensional animation, also called stop-motion animation, depends on taking successive pictures of a subject that is moved very slightly before each shot. The subject might be a toy car, a mass of clay, a model figure based around an articulated skeleton or an actor standing in a series of stationary poses which, when run together, make it look like he is walking.

Animating a simple object can be fun but it's ultimately pretty limiting; there's only so much that can be done. Animating a person (a process known as 'pixillation') is time consuming and looks pretty unrealistic, and is rarely used, and then only for comic effect. But with models the technique comes into its own. The animator can do simple things, like making the model move around, and more subtle things, for example making it express emotions by changing its facial expressions (if it has a face) or by means of body language (i.e. the way it stands and the gestures used). Often the animator uses his body as a template – if the model has to raise its hand and scratch its forehead then the animator times himself performing that action, sees how many frames of film that equates to, and then works out where the hand needs to be in each frame.

Models for animation can be constructed from all kinds of materials. Morph – the little animated figure who used to invade Tony Hart's studio in *The Amazing Adventures of Morph* (1980) – was made entirely of Plasticine which meant that the animators could mould him into any shape they liked. They could turn him, for instance, from a human figure into a long worm-like streak, then into a sphere which could flatten into a disc before making him human again. The animals in the original *Creature Comforts* were also made entirely of Plasticine, but they had little bead-like eyes that could be moved in different directions.

More sophisticated models have a metal armature, like a skeleton, with joints to help the limbs bend. It can be surrounded with padding and covered with a rubbery substance called latex to simulate skin. Slightly less sophisticated models have bodies made entirely of latex, covering the armature while the arms, hands and face are Plasticine. Wallace and Gromit are sometimes made this way.

The models can't exist in limbo, though (although Morph often did). They invariably need a setting which means that suitably sized sets have to be built. And they're usually quite small since most stop-motion models are just 15-30cm (6–12in) high. This is mainly because smaller, lighter models are less likely to droop or fall over.

Because stop-motion animation is such a slow, painstaking process, there are certain things that it can't do very well. Water – flowing out of a tap, as a river or down a waterfall – is particularly tricky. One solution has been to use crinkled cellophane to represent a river, and glycerine has been used to represent raindrops trickling down a window. Smoke is another problem, but cotton wool can be quite convincing. Fire, though, is generally avoided wherever possible.

Another tricky problem involves figures or objects flying through the air. Making a model walk is easy enough – just place one foot in front of

"I can't do with sputum and I can't do very much with feet . . ."

Binky the performing dog

Wallace's amazing Soccamatic machine – one of the many inventions from *Wallace and Gromit's Cracking Contraptions*.

another – but what if the model has to trip and fall over? The answer is usually that the model is supported by a strut (or 'rigging'), usually hidden behind the model, unseen by the camera, attached to a piece of the set. All just tricks of the trade.

What is clear from this description is the sheer painstaking craft involved in the process of stop-motion animation. You don't need many materials to achieve a decent effect – a camera and some Plasticine is about it – but you do need a lot of patience. Stop-motion animators therefore need to be an odd mix of the practical and the creative: they need to concentrate on the small movements of arms and legs for days on end, while simultaneously having the vision and creative flair to envisage the final result. There aren't that many people who can equally balance the two opposing requirements necessary to make a good stop-motion animator, and Aardman employs most of the good ones. And most of them are working on *Creature Comforts*…

the history of stop-motion animation

Introduction

Stop-motion animation has always fascinated children and film-buffs in a way that traditional 2-dimensional animation has never managed. It's clear why. 2-dimensional animation of the Disney type requires the ability to draw recognizable characters and backgrounds. Stop-motion animation merely requires the ability to move a model by a few millimetres and take a photograph. It's the difference between a talent and a skill. Most of us know that we could never make *The Sleeping Beauty* (1959) or *The Lion King* (1994), but we can imagine building a little man out of Plasticine and making him wave.

The technique has been around, and remained almost untouched, for over a century. If you placed one of the pioneers of stop-motion animation in the Aardman studios in Bristol he'd be right at home, if slightly fazed by the multi-coloured Plasticine because way back they actually had to make their own modelling clay.

Early Days

Tracking the early history of some inventions can be difficult because different people might have developed the same technique at the same time. Who gets the credit as The Inventor? With stop-motion animation, we don't know who to name. All we know is that the earliest film containing elements of stop-motion animation may have been *The Humpty Dumpty Circus*, dating back to approximately 1898. It was made by James Stuart Blackton and Albert E. Smith, two stage entertainers who quickly recognized the possibilities of the new technique. Blackton said that he used 'my little daughter's set of toy wooden circus performers and animals, whose movable joints enabled us to place them in balanced positions. It was a tedious process in as much as movement could be achieved only by photographing separately each change of position.'

Ironically, Blackton's associate, Albert E. Smith, wanted to copyright the process but Blackton demurred believing that it was just a parlour trick with no real future. (If Smith had managed to persuade him, or if he'd just had a little more foresight, then there might well be no *Creature Comforts*.) Blackton was one of the pioneers of cinematography, as well as one of the pioneers of animation, and made almost fifty films from 1900–1933. A later film, *The Haunted Hotel* (1907), mixed stop-motion animation with actors in the tale of a traveller exploring a haunted hotel at night, encountering strange phenomena including floating furniture and bread being sliced by an invisible hand.

A convincing case has been made for Blackton and Smith being the first to use stop-motion animation, but most of their films – including, sadly, both *The Humpty Dumpty Circus* and *The Haunted Hotel* – have now vanished, and the dates when they were made are uncertain. But according to other accounts, Arthur Melbourne Cooper may have been the first to develop stop-motion animation. He produced a short piece with moving matchsticks in 1899 for the match manufacturers Bryant and May, while his films *Noah's Ark* (c. 1906) and *Dreams of Toyland* (c. 1908) used toys as their models. Cooper went on to make a number of similar films over the next few years.

Edwin S. Porter is the next contender. He directed the one-minute film, *Fun in a Bakery Shop* (1902), which mixed live action and clay animation, as did his later *A Sculptor's Welsh Rarebit Dream* (1908). All of which means that the best guess is that a number of inventive people involved in the film industry discovered the process more or less independently, at more or less the same time, and it's difficult now, one hundred years on, to say who crossed the line first.

For the next twenty years or so, stop-motion animation was just a novelty, an entertainment along the lines of sleight-of-hand tricks performed by a stage magician. During this time, the most interesting figure was perhaps Ladislaw Starewicz, an Eastern European animator who made a series of short films using embalmed beetles, grasshoppers and dragonflies as his characters.

The use of embalmed insects, as seen here in *The Cameraman's Revenge* by Ladislaw Starewicz, became a hallmark of the pioneering puppet animator. Image courtesy of the BFI.

The period from roughly 1900–1920 can be regarded as a time of experimentation, when the various pioneers in the field were discovering which techniques worked and which didn't, though many of those early films are now lost. From 1920 onwards, however, stop-motion animation became more commercial and more integrated into general film making instead of being seen as special and unusual. It was, by and large, attempting to make people believe that the events depicted were real, rather than drawing attention to the fact that they patently weren't. And for that reason it's convenient to divide the various films (on cinema and TV) over the next seventy years or so into several themes, including dinosaurs, aliens, fantasy and children's films.

Dinosaurs

Mention stop-motion animation to most people of a certain age and they will immediately think of prehistoric animals. Kids are fascinated by them. What did they really look like? How did they move? What colour were they? Until *Jurassic Park* (1993) and *Walking With Dinosaurs* (1999), stop-motion animation was the only method that let people see them as 'real' walking, eating, fighting creatures because it was the only technique that could actually bring them to life. Pretending that iguanas were dinosaurs, as some films did, didn't count.

The Lost World (1924) was a film version of the Arthur Conan Doyle novel of the same name in which dinosaurs are discovered alive and well on a South American plateau. The dinosaurs were created by special effects technician Willis O'Brien, whose name is writ large in movie history for reasons that we will shortly come to. He had been using stop-motion techniques for ten years or so prior to *The Lost World*, and had already made a number of short pieces for The Edison Company.

For reasons that probably had more to do with the crudity of the technique than anything else, it was nearly a decade before the next film involving stop-motion was made. The film was *King Kong* (1933), which immortalized the giant ape and the technique that brought him

'SEE the living, fighting monsters of Creation's dawn, rediscovered in the world today!
King Kong publicity

to life. O'Brien not only created the ape but the various dinosaurs that inhabit Skull Island (and, in a scene that was cut from the final version, a giant spider as well). The film was so popular that a sequel – *Son of Kong* – was quickly rushed into production for release the same year.

Willis O'Brien's next film – *Mighty Joe Young* (1949) – was a kind of stripped down version of Kong with a smaller ape and no dinosaurs, but it did manage to act as a kind of baton-passing, with Willis O'Brien employing the young Ray Harryhausen as his assistant. Harryhausen went on to create an invented dinosaur – a rhedosaurus – for *The Beast From 20,000 Fathoms* (1953), and a giant octopus for *It Came From Beneath the Sea* (1955). In an attempt to cut down the animation workload on the octopus he decided to give it just six tentacles!

The Beast of Hollow Mountain (1956) included a prehistoric creature that went round killing cattle in contemporary Mexico. The script was based on a story by Willis O'Brien, who was going to provide the

The dinosaurs in Willis O'Brien's *The Lost World* were crude compared to some of his later work. © First National, courtesy of the Kobal Collection.

animation effects, but in the end the creature was brought to life by a rag-bag of techniques. They included a stop-motion animation technique in which different models were used for each frame of film, instead of the one model being repositioned for each frame.

Willis O'Brien did, however, work on *The Black Scorpion* (1957) and *The Giant Behemoth* (1959), but they weren't his finest moments. The dinosaur that devastates London in *The Giant Behemoth* was constructed so cheaply that the seams are visible up its neck!

The period from 1956–1961 was an obviously fallow one for stop-motion animation. Despite the fact that the creatures in *Dinosaurus!* (1960) were built by Marcel Delgado, the same craftsman who had built King Kong for Willis O'Brien, the models were crude and silly, and the standard of the animation didn't help. In the end it was Ray Harryhausen who rescued the reputation of stop-motion animation in *Mysterious Island* (1961), when he produced a giant chambered nautilus (like a squid in a shell) and a phorohacos (a giant bird), giant wasps and a giant crab. The animation is excellent – Harryhausen obviously had plenty of time – and the film stands up well to repeat viewing.

King Kong's son confronts a miniature dinosaur in *Son of Kong*. © RKO, courtesy of the Kobal Collection.

Harryhausen's next two films were fantasy and science fiction, but he returned to animating dinosaurs in what is, perhaps, the classic dinosaur movie, *One Million Years BC* (1966). His creations for that film were unsurpassed for almost thirty years, until *Jurassic Park*. Harryhausen's last dinosaur movie – *The Valley of Gwangi* (1969) – was a come-down in comparison, with cowboys chasing after a confused allosaurus in New Mexico.

Dinosaur movies went into something of a decline over the next twenty years. Apart from a humorous interlude in *Naked Gun 33⅓* (1994) in which a stop-motion creature turns and laughs at the camera in the title sequence, there was very little worth mentioning. It was difficult to improve on Ray Harryhausen's seminal efforts. And, of course, when Steven Spielberg came to film Michael Crichton's novel *Jurassic Park*, he broke ranks and used a completely different technique – computer-generated images.

25

Science Fiction

For many years the only things that were created in movies using stop-motion animation were dinosaurs, big apes and toys with a life of their own. It took some years for the realization to sink in that other things could be animated as well. And that's when Ray Harryhausen used his familiar techniques to create aliens from outer space.

Below left: Miniature AT-AT Walkers from *Star Wars: The Empire Strikes Back*. For long shots, smaller models give a false sense of scale.

Rather bizarrely, however, in his first attempt at science fiction – *Earth Versus the Flying Saucers* (1956) – he was responsible not for the alien creatures but for their spacecraft. He did provide a Venusian monster running riot through Rome in *20 Million Miles to Earth* (1957), though for the next few years he turned his attention to more fantastic

Above right: An AT-AT Walker crumples to the ground in *Star Wars: The Empire Strikes Back*. The model is supported in its pose by plenty of rigging. © Lucasfilm/ 20th Century Fox, courtesy of the Kobal Collection.

and mythological worlds. Harryhausen returned to science fiction for the final time in 1964, with *First Men in the Moon*, a light-hearted romp in which he provided numerous insectoid inhabitants from the moon and examples of their oversized technology. For over a decade, science fiction and stop-motion animation then went their separate ways.

The release of *Star Wars* (1977) kick-started a new interest in stop-motion animation, just as *King Kong* had done 44 years before. George Lucas plundered an entire toolbox of techniques in order to develop the special effects for his epic science-fiction film, and his original intention had been to use stop-motion techniques to provide a number of creatures for the Tatooine desert planet scenes (including a stop-motion animated Jabba the Hutt). But it proved too expensive and time consuming and, in the end, stop-motion animation was limited to a few brief moments when alien chess pieces moved in the match between

R2-D2 and Chewbacca. The work was done by animator Phil Tippett, who returned for more extensive work on *The Empire Strikes Back* (1980) when he animated the Tauntaun creatures on the ice-planet of Hoth, and the elephantine Imperial AT-AT Walkers that attacked the rebel base in the film's early scenes. Tippett also animated the two-legged AT-ST Walkers in *Return of the Jedi* (1983), his work providing a number of key dramatic scenes and a comedy moment when one of the Walkers steps on a rolling log, during a climactic battle scene, and staggers drunkenly around, attempting to regain its balance, before collapsing and exploding.

But the writing was already on the wall for stop-motion animation. Both *Tron* (1982) and *The Last Starfighter* (1984) had used extensive

computer-generated effects, and it didn't take a genius to realize that the days of stop-motion animation for anything realistic were numbered. Phil Tippett went on to provide a wacky alien creature for *Howard the Duck* (1986), and various robots for the three *Robocop* movies – ED-209 in *Robocop* (1987), the villainous Cain in *Robocop 2* (1990), and the welcome return of ED-209 in *Robocop 3* (1993) – before broadening his portfolio to include CGI as well.

One or two films kept the stop-motion flag flying, usually the ones where animators were prepared to work cheap in return for a credit and something which they could use to demonstrate their expertise. *Robot Jox* (1991) and *Robot Wars* (1993) both involved massive robot creatures created by the magic of stop-motion animation, but neither made more than a slight ripple in the pool of film history. Essentially, stop-motion animation was dead for any projects apart from those that actually wanted

An AT-AT Walker approaches the Rebel Base in *Star Wars: The Empire Strikes Back*. The AT-AT design was based on an elephant's body, with elongated, Dali-esque legs. © Lucasfilm/20th Century Fox, courtesy of the Kobal Collection.

to *look* stop-motion animated. The final nail in its coffin was Tim Burton's decision, during pre-production for *Mars Attacks!* (1996), to junk all the work that had been done on hundreds of stop-motion animated Martians and replace them with CGI ones.

Children's Animation

It was George Pal – the same man who went on to make *War of the Worlds* (1953) – who developed stop-motion animation for children. He started in the 1930s with a series of what he called 'Puppetoons', and for ten years or so he made many short films, some semi-realistic and others, like *Tubby the Tuba* (1947), more fantastic. Pal also employed various animators in his studio who went on to bigger and better things, including Ray Harryhausen.

However, the story of contemporary – or near contemporary – stop-motion animation for children is really the story of four different talents: Serge Danot in France and, from the UK, Oliver Postgate and Peter Firmin (of Smallfilms), Cosgrove Hall, and the Gordon Murray-Bob Bura-and-John Hardwick trio.

Serge Danot was the man responsible for BBC's *The Magic Roundabout* (1965–1977) though he never became as famous as Eric Thompson (the father of actress Emma Thompson), who provided the voices for all the characters when the series came to the UK, and who changed the plots and characters willy-nilly. We might not know what the original French series was like, but Eric Thompson's version became legendary with its group of disparate characters including Dougall the dog, Dylan the rabbit, Brian the snail and the bizarre, springing up-and-down Zebedee, all set in a world of cut-out trees and flowers. *The Magic Roundabout* captivated an entire generation from the mid-1960s, and then another in 1992 when fifty-two episodes that had previously never made it to the UK were brought over, with Nigel Planer doing the voices in the same style. The animation was crude but effective, and the characters were individuals with plenty of quirks. Dougall zipped about like a hyperactive child, while Dylan stumbled around like the world's hippiest hippy, and Zebedee... well, he bounced.

Smallfilms, in contrast, was a British venture, almost the Aardman Animations of its day. It began in the mid-1960s with *Pingwings*, simple tales about simple penguins, and then moved to more sophisticated fare in the late 1960s and early 1970s with *Ivor the Engine*, *The Pogles* and its spin-off, *Pogle's Wood*, before hitting the big time with *The Clangers* (1969-1974) and *Bagpuss* (1974). *The Clangers* was about a group of knitted alien creatures who lived on what looked like a very small asteroid, with a soup dragon, music trees and some frog-like creatures, while *Bagpuss* was about a cloth cat and his toy friends who came alive every night and told stories. *The Clangers*, like *The Magic Roundabout*, has almost become a definition of what children's television should be – fun and full of odd characters with added levels that people of any age can appreciate. With *The Magic Roundabout* and *Bagpuss* it is as much a part of the 1960s as are The Beatles, Mods and Rockers, and the first spacemen. In many ways *The Clangers* prefigures what Aardman did with *Wallace and Gromit* when it created television that both kids and adults could enjoy – albeit for different reasons.

With models built by Gordon Murray and animated by Bob Bura and John Hardwick, the *Trumpton* trilogy is the third leg of the platform of stop-motion animated children's programmes in the 1960s and 1970s, the platform upon which Aardman have built. *Camberwick Green* (1966), *Trumpton* (1967) and *Chigley* (1969) were a linked series of episodes set in the same rural location, with some of the same characters turning up in various programmes. Like the other children's programmes mentioned, the animation was pretty crude but it did

Below, left and middle: Cosgrove Hall's animated version of The Wind in the Willows is a classic of the form. Bottom right: Count Duckula – another work of art from Cosgrove Hall. © Fremantle Media Enterprises.

Above right: The Clangers is still popular with children today.
Opposite: The saggy old cloth cat named Bagpuss. © Licensing by Design.

conjure up a world of its own, a world of firemen named Pugh, Pugh, Barney McGrew, Cuthbert, Dibble and Grub, a world of Windy Miller and Roger Varley the chimney sweep.

Cosgrove Hall is a company that has worked equally successfully in 2-dimensional and 3-dimensional animation. Its 2-dimensional work includes *Dangermouse* (1981) and *Count Duckula* (1988), and its 3-dimensional credits are topped by classics such as *Chorlton and the Wheelies* (1976-1979) and *The Wind in the Willows* (1983).

There have been many other, terrific animated children's series from the 1970s onwards, notably *Paddington* (1975), *The Wombles* (1974 and 1998), *Noddy* (1975 and onwards), and *The Trap Door* (1985), a personal favourite of Nick Park, but none has quite managed the same level of familiarity and longevity as those early ones. And sadly, now, most of the new series are being made using computer-generated animation. It's a great shame because the simplicity of the early programmes got a big response from kids.

Horror

Interestingly, stop-motion animation aimed specifically at kids tended to stay on TV, whereas stop-motion animation aimed at family audiences and adults tended to stay on the cinema screens. This was primarily

because it's a complicated, time-consuming and expensive process, and movies could afford better animation than TV. And kids, it was felt, were more likely to accept the relatively crude animation which was all that TV could afford.

The number of films containing stop-motion animation that was aimed specifically at kids was small. An honourable exception was *Dougall and the Blue Cat* (1972), a spin-off from the French TV series, but from then until *The Nightmare Before Christmas* (1993) there is a dearth of products. And even that *Nightmare* film – directed and animated by Henry Selick, but produced by Tim Burton – had a sly eye on the adult market while it marketed itself as a dark Christmas fable. Selick's next film, *James and the Giant Peach* (1996), was a more commercial adaptation of a Roald Dahl story. As with *The Nightmare Before Christmas*, Selick made life difficult for himself by animating his characters to speak *and* sing. Stop-motion musicals? Hardly. In Selick's latest film, *Monkeybone* (2001), he mixes various techniques including stop-motion animation, CGI and live action to tell the story of a cartoonist who gets sucked into the world of his own creation when he falls into a coma.

Mention of Tim Burton leads one inexorably to the area where horror and dark fantasy meet. Now there haven't been many horror movies with stop-motion animation for several good reasons. First, most horror films are made quickly, and stop-motion animation takes a long time. And second, most horror films strive for realism and immediacy whereas there's always something a little bit false and distancing about the stop-motion process. Having said that, some horror films have used the technique to show cinema-goers the kind of monsters that couldn't be produced using latex, as happened in horror novelist Clive Barker's directorial debut *Nightbreed* (1990).

The combination of Tim Burton's gothic imagination and Henry Selick's animation wizardry turned *The Nightmare Before Christmas* into a visual treat. © Paramount, courtesy of the Kobal Collection.

Opposite: Jack Skellington and Sally share a romantic moment in *The Nightmare Before Christmas*. © Paramount, courtesy of the Kobal Collection.

It's also an area that the animator Dave Allen made his own until his untimely death in 1999. Having created a reptilian beast that's worshipped by the Aztecs in *Q-The Winged Serpent* (1982), he then produced deadly dolls and puppets for a slew of low-budget horror movies in the *Puppetmaster* series (five films from 1989–95), and the *Dolls* and *Demonic Toys* series (four films from 1987–93). He also created small but vicious reptilian beasts for the *Subspecies* films (three of them from 1991–93). As you can tell, he worked fast.

Tim Burton is one of cinema's few current *auteur* directors. His dark humour and askance view of life are evident in most of his films, and it's no surprise to find that he loves the idea of stop-motion animation. One of his first attempts at film-making – a short piece called *Vincent* (1982) – used the technique to tell the story of a boy who thought he was horror film actor Vincent Price. He returned to the technique briefly in his breakthrough movie, *Beetlejuice* (1988), in order to provide huge sandworms and sculptures that come to life.

Following the musical fantasy *The Nightmare Before Christmas*, Burton briefly toyed with the idea of stop-motion to animate several hundred big-brained Martians for *Mars Attacks!*, but he soon realized that computer-generated imagery had developed to the point where he could now use it to do everything he wanted and more, far quicker and better. It was the death knell for serious stop-motion animation.

More spooky creatures – Lock, Shock and Barrel – from *The Nightmare Before Christmas*. © Paramount, courtesy of the Kobal Collection.

Fantasy

Stop-motion animation was a godsend for fantasy movies, and vice-versa. Myths and legends have always been at the heart of storytelling, and having a way of bringing them to life suddenly added a whole new dimension to the cinematic art. Previously men in rubber suits had to play aliens, and dinosaurs were created by sticking bits of rubber on small reptiles, but dragons were another matter. And so were animated skeletons.

One of the first, and one of the best fantasy films to use stop-motion animation was *The Seventh Voyage of Sinbad* (1958). The first of a loose trilogy of films concerning the adventures of the courageous captain from *The Arabian Nights* (a series of tales dating from around the 10th century AD) the film had special effects provided by the ever-reliable Ray Harryhausen. A dragon, a skeleton battling with a sword, and a massive cyclops – these things had never been seen before. Or not as shown here, at any rate.

The same year, *Tom Thumb* provided cinema-goers with a stop-motion animated set of nursery toys, animated by Wah Chung and Gene Warren, while *Jack the Giant Killer* (1961) reminded them of why dragons and animation go so well together. Ray Harryhausen's skills were

Ray Harryhausen's Cyclops from *The Seventh Voyage of Sinbad* – special effects didn't get any better than this in the early 1970s. © Columbia Pictures, courtesy of the Kobal Collection.

demonstrated once again in *Jason and the Argonauts* (1963), where he went one better than before and produced an entire battalion of fighting skeletons, as well as flying harpies and another dragon.

All that good work was undermined by *The Seven Faces of Dr Lao* (1964) which managed to set the cause of animation back several years with its crudely realized sea serpent (courtesy of Jim Danforth), which meant that for a while stop-motion and fantasy went their separate ways. Things didn't pick up again until 1973 when Ray Harryhausen returned to the genre with *The Golden Voyage of Sinbad,* in which he

One of cinema's classic moments – Jason battles the children of the Hydra's teeth in Jason and the Argonauts – another example of back-projection being used to tie live action and animation together. © Columbia Pictures, courtesy of the Kobal Collection.

topped even his previous best efforts by presenting us with a six-armed Indian goddess of death with a sword in each hand. *Sinbad and the Eye of the Tiger* (1977) was a lesser effort, although it is the only known film to date to use a giant walrus as a monster. It's also one of the first films to use a stop-motion animated creation – in this case, a baboon – as a sympathetic character who communicates with the other characters in the film, and not as a monster or a threat.

Ray Harryhausen's latest film to date is *Clash of the Titans* (1981) in which Perseus has to save Andromeda from the clutches of a monstrous sea creature. But it marks a low point in Harryhausen's career because he had to animate a mechanical owl in a forlorn attempt to appeal to a post-*Star Wars* audience.

The only major fantasy film to use the specialist skills of the stop-motion animator since *Clash of the Titans* has been *Willow* (1988). Set in a world of heroes and villains, and monsters and magic, Phil Tippett used the skills he'd learned on *Star Wars*, *The Empire Strikes Back* and *Return of the Jedi* to create a bizarre two-headed chicken monster. Tippett was also the man behind the creatures in *Dragonslayer* (1981) which used a technique close to stop-motion animation.

Fantasy has been something of a dead genre since then. Dragons are now brought to life using computers – but then again, what isn't?

Serious Stop-Motion

The majority of stop-motion animation from the 1930s until now has been of fantastical things, such as dragons, dinosaurs and aliens, but often placed in real settings. There is, however, an alternative European (not American) tradition, in which the technique is used to more artistic ends, with the animated subjects being closer to toys or puppets, being intended to represent human beings, or having no direct equivalent in the real world.

Ladislaw Starewicz, an early Polish animator who had achieved success making films by posing embalmed insects in various positions, went on to produce a number of short films with elements of fantasy,

A horned Neanderthal confronts a sabre-toothed tiger, courtesy of Ray Harryhausen, in *Sinbad and the Eye of the Tiger*. Fur is always difficult in stop-motion animation. © Columbia Pictures, courtesy of the Kobal Collection.

including *The Mascot* (1934). Its story of toys on a quest descends into a hellish episode involving devil dolls and a macabre, mummified figure.

Jiri Trnka, a Czechoslovakian animator, used the same techniques as George Pal (who developed stop-motion animation for children in the 1930s) about the same time. But Jiri used them in conjunction with elements of fairy tale, literature and even political satire in order to present striking short films such as *A Midsummer Night's Dream* (1955) and *The Hand* (1965). A group of Russian animators (including Stanislav Sokolov, Maria Muat and Galina Beda, collectively known as Christmas Films) also turned to Shakespeare when they produced animated versions of *The Tempest* and *Twelfth Night* (both 1992) for the BBC and S4C, as well as various Biblical tales given the overall title *Testament* (1996).

Possibly the most extreme living stop-motion animator is the Czech Jan Svankmajer, whose disturbing clay figures could be found during the mid-1980s gracing the late night BBC2 schedules. Svankmajer's films include such grotesque images as two clay heads perpetually eating and regurgitating each other, various bodily parts gradually assembling themselves into a human being who is then trapped inside a small box, and a baby with an oversized skull instead of a head in *Faust*

(1994). His themes have been picked up by the Quay Brothers, a pair of identical twins, born in America but working in Britain. Besides producing a documentary about their former mentor, they have created a number of short films – including *Nocturna Artificialia* (1979) and *The Street of Crocodiles* (1986) – with the same disturbing power of Svankmajer but seen through a filter of dusty childhood memories. The Quay Brothers were also involved in creating the video for Peter Gabriel's song *Sledgehammer*, with Nick Park and Aardman Animations.

Top: Jiri Trnka's disconcerting film *The Hand*. Image courtesy of the BFI. Opposite: A lot to animate in *The Tempest*; above: Minstrels and a jester from *Twelfth Night*; and bottom: *Testament*. All courtesy of S4C.

Conclusion

Above: Prospero and
Caliban play their
games in *The Tempest*,
courtesy of S4C.
Opposite: Wallace and
Gromit think the
Cardomatic machine
has solved all of their
Christmas problems in
*Wallace and Gromit's
Cracking Contraptions*.
How wrong they are...

2-dimensional animation has been pigeon-holed primarily as a medium
for children, despite the best efforts of pioneers like Ralph Bakshi and
Bill Plympton in the 1980s. Stop-motion animation, which was invented
about the same time, hasn't suffered the same fate. To a large extent
this is because it's not amenable to the same production-line techniques
that companies such as Disney and DreamWorks SKG have applied to
it. (It's also worth noting that with 2-dimensional animation it's possible
for the style of the individual animator to get lost in the mix. With stop-
motion the animator often *is* the animation because his gestures,
movements and body language are built in from the start.)

In fact, most of the big 2-dimensional animation projects are
now either farmed out to animation factories in the Far East – Disney's
The Tigger Movie, for instance (2000), and TV's *The Simpsons* (from
1989) – or are created in whole or in part inside a computer –*Treasure
Planet* (2003), and *Final Fantasy: The Spirit Within* (2001). It's hard, in
fact, almost impossible, to imagine hundreds of Korean animators
working on Plasticine models of Wallace and Gromit. Fortunately, the
unique work produced by Aardman Animations is likely to continue
for many years to come.

Part Two: The Origins of Creature Comforts

the history of aardman

There's something curiously British about the fact that one of our best-known and most successful TV and film companies – with a five-movie deal with Steven Spielberg's production company, DreamWorks SKG – was formed by two school-friends with a joint hobby. You can't really imagine that kind of thing happening in Los Angeles where power breakfasts and executive meetings are the order of the day. In the early days of Aardman Animations, the closest the two founders ever got to a power breakfast was the school canteen.

David Sproxton and Peter Lord sat side by side in a classroom in Woking, back in the mid-1960s. They became close friends, a closeness forged in part by a shared interest in film. 'We were two schoolboy hobbyists,' David Sproxton says. 'My father happened to be in the BBC as a producer, and we had a 16mm Bolex in the family.'

They spent weekends learning how to use it, and soon discovered that they could produce interesting effects not by filming the real world but by creating short, animated pieces. 'It's interesting,' Peter says, 'because we did contemplate live action. We had a location, which was this derelict house in Walton on Thames, and we had the camera, but we never made the film.'

It would be tempting to say that both Peter and David had always nurtured a burning desire to be animators. What actually happened was that someone suggested that they try animation and, as Peter says, 'We did and thought "Wow, this is great! This is such fun!"'

'I was always keen on photography and lighting,' explains David Sproxton. 'Peter had story and drawing skills, so animation seemed to be the way forward.' They began by mounting the camera vertically, looking down at a blackboard on the kitchen table, and drawing a figure

'Wow, this is great! This is such fun!'

Peter Lord

in chalk on the board. They exposed one frame of film, then wiped out a part of the figure (for example an arm or leg) and redrew it in a different position. Eventually they had a series of 16mm-pictures which, when shown at the rate of twenty-four frames per second, showed the chalk figure moving in a realistic manner. The technique immediately appealed to the two school kids. 'With live action it seems hugely different and complicated,' Peter explains, 'whereas in animation you feel you can just hold the whole world in your hand.'

They continued their experiments, extending their technique from chalk drawings to line drawings on transparent plastic film, the same technique used then (and now) by Disney and its competitors. They animated model cars which were moved bit by bit, photo by photo, in front of a camera, and, eventually, used Plasticine which was gradually sculpted into different shapes. They were helped in their efforts by the gift of 30m (100ft) of unexposed film by one of David's dad's colleagues at the BBC who had been impressed by their results.

David Sproxton (left) and Peter Lord (right) demonstrate some of their early models.

47

One of the 2-dimensional animations completed by the boys involved a gormless superhero in a skin-tight costume; a character created by Peter for a cartoon strip some time before. The piece only lasted for twenty-five seconds but, unexpectedly, the BBC offered them £15 for it, and showed it on their *Vision On* series of programmes in the 1970s.

For such a short piece, the preparation was immense. 'I think it took about a week,' Peter remembers. 'I can't imagine we had the patience for much more than that. We were doing it totally on the cheap and without any equipment or, indeed, knowledge. So the animation wasn't very good and we didn't know which pens to use to trace with, and we didn't know which paint to use. And we made a camera rostrum to hang the camera on, in fact it was all hand-made. It seemed like very hard work and wasn't satisfying.'

But suddenly that £15 payment meant that their hobby had turned into a fledgling business, and they had to open a bank account. Fittingly, they named the account in honour of their gormless superhero.

'It was just a schoolboy joke,' Peter recalls. 'When they said, "Who do we make the cheque out to?," we toyed with Super Animation Productions, and World of Animation, and Pete and Dave Animation… and settled on Aardman. Actually joke was too strong a word! It just seemed quite funny – the word was just a combination of aardvark and Superman.'

Peter Lord and David Sproxton's laid-back superhero, Aardman.

'We did Aardman for one year, I think,' Peter remembers. 'It was a hard slog and not very satisfactory. We were doing what everyone else was doing, but not very well. In fact we were doing rather bad animation. And then we started working with Plasticine and suddenly we were doing something that nobody else was doing, and that was great. With our previous work, people were merely polite. But when we started working with Plasticine, they got really enthusiastic.'

They provided material for *Vision On* for about four years, having started when they were at school and continued through university. 'But just when we'd finished university and were ready for a career, they axed *Vision On* and turned it into *Take Hart*,' says Peter. 'That was a bad moment but, after a while, they came back and luckily said they wanted something for the new programme. Which, now I think about it, was really lucky because if they hadn't, that would have been it. We'd have probably jacked it in there and then.'

They didn't and, what's more, *Take Hart* gave them the opportunity to create a regular character for the series. 'He didn't have a name to start with,' says Peter, 'but he just became Morph – I would say he evolved from a lump of Plasticine over a short period.'

'The word was just a combination of aardvark and Superman.'
Peter Lord

Morph, the smooth-skinned little figure with the spherical head and the incomprehensible voice, quickly captured the imaginations of millions of children. He was a real character with a real personality. Animated 3-dimensional characters made of rigid materials can only express a limited range of emotions. Morph's clay body, and the skill of his animators, meant that he could be angry, happy, confrontational, chirpy, puzzled, sad, tired... almost anything that was required.

'If you take *The Wombles*, say, which I like very much, they're lovely characters, but they're remarkably inexpressive,' Peter explains. 'If Morph slumps down miserably, because he's all Plasticine you can make his shoulders slump and you can make his spine curve the wrong way, and you can make his limbs look very, very heavy. With those more conventional puppets, you can't do that.'

Peter and David's work with *Vision On* gave them the impetus to get a more serious project off the ground. *Animated Conversations* (1978) consisted of two, five-minute films, also for the BBC, in which real conversations were placed in the mouths of Plasticine characters. The first, *Confessions of a Foyer Girl*, involved two cinema usherettes talking about their work and their lives. The second, *Down and Out*, was recorded in a Salvation Army hostel.

As Peter recalls, 'Because we were new to the business we tried to get into anything that was going. We made contact with a producer called Colin Thomas from the BBC, who had the eye for *Down and Out*. We sent a sound recordist to the Salvation Army hostel in Bristol, and he hid the microphone and recorded what was said. Yes it was eavesdropping, so we had to find the people afterwards and say, "Hope you don't mind, but we've been recording you, will you sign your rights away for fifteen quid?" or whatever. We recorded for quite a long time, I think three hours, but almost nothing happened. People came in, said "Hello George" and "Here's my money", and went out again. But luckily there was one, five-minute conversation in the middle which I won't say actually made sense, but it was complete. It had a sense of resolution.'

'When we started working with Plasticine, they got really enthusiastic.'

Peter Lord

One of the greats of stop-motion – Morph – contemplates the world from beside his very own (home made) movie camera.

Animated Conversations: Confessions of a Foyer Girl (note the holes in the beads used for eyes).

Initially, the plan had been to take advantage of the nature of Plasticine and produce a kind of fantasy film but, as Peter explains, things didn't work out that way. 'At first we tried to make it very cartoonish, so that when a guy said "I need a bath" we'd have him turn into a bath. But Colin Thomas said, "That doesn't look very good. Why don't you just try doing it straight?"'

In a way, what David and Peter were doing with *Animated Conversations* was what the French surrealist Marcel Duchamp (1887–1968) had previously done when he invented the medium of *objets trouvés* or 'found objects' by taking something that was lying around and transforming it into a work of art. But instead of using Duchamp's urinals they worked with conversation.

In these early days of Aardman, they were more or less learning on the job. Peter remembers that, on *Animated Conversations,* 'Our first ever Plasticine puppet was about four inches tall. We were quite pleased with ourselves because we found glass eyes at the market for teddy bears, and stuck these in its head. Morph had previously had Plasticine eyes, and we thought these teddy bear glittering eyes would be a big improvement. But they weren't round, they were semi-flat and didn't move. We made the model blink a couple of times and these horrible eyes just sat there in his head. That was the most scary thing – the

eyes were absolutely lacking in life. It was horrible to watch. The lower half of the face had a life of its own and it was really offensive to the eye.'

The solution to the problem of providing a model with realistic eyes is one that's still in use today on *Creature Comforts*. As Peter says: 'Somebody suggested using beads, sticking them in the head so that the eye could move – when the character talked the eye could look right at the other person or just dart off for a minute and then move back, or just drop the eye line a bit.

'It was much less tricky but equally effective when we had this character who wiped his nose – he actually ran his finger casually under his nose. And when we screened that everyone shrieked with laughter. They said, "That's so clever" but it wasn't that clever, it's just that no-one else had thought of animating those little things that people often don't even know they're doing.'

The pair got little feedback from the BBC about *Animated Conversations* but Jeremy Isaacs, who was in the process of setting up the new Channel 4, had seen the films.

Two from *Conversation Pieces* – above from *Late Edition*, left from *On Probation*.

'If Morph slumps down miserably, because he's all Plasticine you can make his shoulders slump and you can make his spine curve the wrong way, and you can make his limbs look very, very heavy.'

Peter Lord

Opposite: *The Adventures of Morph.*

As David Sproxton explains: 'We'd sent a bundle of ideas up to Channel 4 on our show reel, and that was on it. We were talking to the commissioning editor, and Jeremy Isaacs came into the room and said, "I've just seen that film *Down and Out* and can I have ten of them for the first week of transmission please?" And that was our first commission.'

Isaacs commissioned a similar project, called *Conversation Pieces*, from Aardman. This was to consist of five separate pieces, each lasting five minutes. David and Peter again directed and animated the models because they were still the only two people in the company. The pieces were entitled *On Probation* (with a probation officer talking to a young offender), *Sales Pitch* (a door-to-door salesman flogging cleaning equipment), *Palmy Days* (a group of elderly people discussing their travel experiences), *Early Bird* (a morning radio show) and *Late Edition* (a day in the life of a local listings magazine), and they were shown late at night.

'We tried hiding microphones in several locations,' says Peter, 'to record real conversations for the films. One was an ironmonger's shop, but the material was no good. We tried one in a barber's shop, but the same thing happened. In fact one of the customer's in the chair spotted the microphone and said, "Here, what's that?" and there was quite a barney.'

Although nobody knew it at the time, the *Palmy Days* episode set the scene for a radical shift in Aardman's output. With the two *Animated Conversations* and four of the five *Conversation Pieces*, David and Peter had tried to replicate the reality of the streets and halls where the conversations had been recorded. But with *Palmy Days* the two of them were concerned that the conversation was so rambling and inconsequential that it lacked any interest at all. In desperation, they let the design of the animation pull against the dialogue by dressing their models in palm leaf skirts and placing them in a tropical island paradise. The result was that the episode stood out well from the rest because the drama came not from the words, but from the obvious discrepancy between what the audience was hearing and seeing.

David Sproxton remembers that: 'At one point we all hoofed off to NY for a summer to work on the *Pee Wee Herman Show*. Golly [Richard Goleszowski] and Nick [Park] lived in one apartment on 22nd Street, and Pete and I lived in another apartment a bit further south.'

Meanwhile, Morph stayed with *Take Hart* until the BBC stopped making the programme. Morph was, however, too popular (and too arrogant) to stay out of the limelight forever and, in 1981, he returned to the BBC for a series of twenty-six, five-minute episodes entitled *The Adventures of Morph*.

But now Aardman was almost hijacked in an entirely unexpected direction. Advertising companies had suddenly latched onto the fact that the output from this tiny, two-man Bristol studio had a liveliness and style

that made it stand out from everything else. Adverts were commissioned, initially one or two, and then an increasing stream. From 1983–1988 Aardman produced only one thing that wasn't an advert or a pop video (a rather more sophisticated advert) – a fourteen-minute satire on the arms industry entitled *Babylon*, which was also for Channel 4.

It was this influx of work that caused the company to expand rapidly. New faces suddenly appeared in what had previously been a two-man operation. Richard Goleszowski joined in 1983, following a short career in graphic design. Nick Park joined in 1985, direct from a course at the National Film and Television School. And more specialized people, non-animators such as cameraman Andy MacCormack, also came on board. All three are still there, twenty or so years later, which says a lot about the kind of loyalty people have to a company named initially after an aardvark and Superman.

When Nick Park arrived he brought with him the project he had started while on his student course, a fantasy about a man and his dog who travel to the moon in search of cheese. Peter and David did provide him with the resources and time to complete the film, which was shown by C4 in 1989 under the title *A Grand Day Out*, but his first task was to

Bottom Left: Wallace and Gromit pose in *A Grand Day Out*.
Bottom Right: A coin-operated inhabitant of the moon in *A Grand Day Out*.

'Everything was simpler then, the company was small, the profits on commercials were high and we were young, carefree and confident.'
Peter Lord

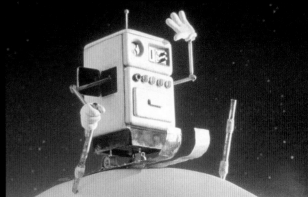

work on a belated follow-up to *Animated Conversations* and *Conversation Pieces* entitled *Lip Synch.*

'Everything was simpler then,' Peter remembers, 'the company was small, the profits on commercials were high and we were young, carefree and confident. So we more or less stopped doing commercials totally for that period and just did this run of films.'

Lip Synch was short for lip synchronization, which is a common TV and film industry phrase for matching an actor's (recorded) voice to the movements of his (filmed) lips. Channel 4 had commissioned *Lip Synch*, and the plan was that the overall series would consist (like *Conversation Pieces*) of five, five-minute episodes, but the brief was much wider and the results more surreal. While Peter's *Going Equipped* and *War Story* were recorded monologues animated with semi-realistic figures, *Next* (by Barry Purves, another new addition to the Aardman roster) had William Shakespeare auditioning in front of a barely interested theatre director, and Richard Goleszowski's *Ident* was based on grotesque figures living under a totalitarian regime. The fifth episode harked back to *Palmy Days* in its juxtaposition of real dialogue and unusual setting. Here, however, it wasn't just the location that was

Above, left to right:
Four aspects of *Lip Synch* – *Next*, *Ident*, *Going Equipped* and *War Story*.
Below left: **Wallace and Gromit capture Fingers McGraw in *The Wrong Trousers*.**
Below right: **Preston displays his skill at handling sheep in *A Close Shave*.**

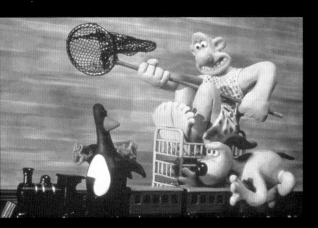

Above, top to bottom: *Wat's Pig*, *Hum Drum*, *Angry Kid*, *Stage Fright*.
Opposite: *Not Without My Handbag*.

changed but the species of the speakers as well. Despite the fact that it was a last minute addition to the Channel 4 proposal, Nick Park's *Creature Comforts* was to be the start of something big.

When Nick Park's *A Grand Day Out* was shown it was a wild, if unexpected success and led to two further films, *The Wrong Trousers* (1993) and *A Close Shave* (1995), starring the same characters and commissioned by the BBC. Meanwhile, Richard Goleszowski had created his own character with the gingerbread dog Rex the Runt, who appeared in two short pieces in 1990 and 1991, and then went on to get his own thirteen-part series in 1998. And there were other one-off animations including *Never Say Pink Furry Die* (1992), *Not Without My Handbag* (1993), *Pib and Pog* (1994), *Pop* (1996), *Wat's Pig* (also 1996, and the last piece of real animation done by Peter Lord), *Stage Fright* (1997) and *Hum Drum* (1998). Many of these were animated and sometimes directed by people brought into Aardman during the late 1980s.

The history of Aardman Animations is not one of a smooth progression from the early days to now. It's actually more like a series of sudden, steep changes followed by periods of rest and consolidation. Which means, of course, that the most recent steep change should actually come as no surprise to anyone.

The release of the full-length movie *Chicken Run* (2000) brought Aardman and its unique productions to a much wider audience than before. The film resulted from a partnership deal with the major Hollywood production company DreamWorks SKG, and was hugely successful in the UK, the USA and right around the world. As a result, Aardman and DreamWorks SKG have since signed a deal to make another four movies, the second of which is likely to be the long-awaited Wallace and Gromit movie.

Refusing to stay still, Aardman is also taking full advantage of the new media, as well as film and TV. A series of short Wallace and Gromit pieces, with the overall title *Wallace and Gromit's Cracking Contraptions*, was shown on the BBC in 2002, following the earlier internet success of Aardman's *Angry Kid*, directed by Darren Walsh. Other projects will no doubt follow. And yet, despite the huge list of things that must be occupying the creative teams at Aardman, despite all the potential and actual projects for the future, it is *Creature Comforts* that is occupying the model makers, the set makers, the lighting riggers and animators during 2003. A long-belated sequel to the most memorable segment of *Lip Synch*, the series will be aired on ITV in late 2003. And if you want some kind of insight into the way the people at Aardman approach their craft (and it is a craft), then delving into the details of *Creature Comforts* is the best place to start...

the original creature comforts

the original creature comforts

This page and opposite: Birds of a species unknown to biological science. Note particularly the way their beaks are held on with elastic.

Like most great art, the original *Creature Comforts* came about through a combination of perfect timing and sheer luck. Although it now seems like a perfect follow-up to their previous work, *Animated Conversations* and *Conversation Pieces*, one can't help wondering how much of its style depended on Nick Park having recently joined the company. Would there be a *Creature Comforts* now if he hadn't?

'When I was at art school,' Nick remembers, 'everyone was talking about *Animated Conversations* and *Conversation Pieces*, which were all about going out and interviewing people and using their voices as the basis for films – documentary-style animation – which was very innovative at the time. I found that particularly attractive. In fact, I invited Peter and David to lecture at the National Film School. They happened to see my work that day, and I got an invite to come and work for them a few months later.'

As Nick remembers, when he joined there was a feeling within the company that it had drifted away from its roots. 'At the time we were doing short films for Channel 4,' he recalls, 'and commercials. There were only about five or six people in the company, and we were hankering to do something a bit more like the old *Animated Conversations*. We all wanted to direct something, and came up with an idea roughly based on *vox-pop* interviews or conversations recorded in a room.'

'I didn't think the fact that I was using animals would particularly stand out.'

Nick Park

From the start, Nick knew the basic theme that he wanted to get people to talk about for his section of *Lip Synch*. 'I was going to go to the zoo and record people chatting about the animals,' he says, 'but it was so hard to get that sort of fly-on-the-wall-stuff, and there was always another loud noise like a fountain or fan blowing. So I thought, Why not just go up to people and ask them what they think?'

The choice of a zoo as the location wasn't exactly a coincidence. 'Nick's a keen ornithologist,' David Sproxton points out. 'Quite keen on natural history.' The problem was, zoos are not exactly benign environments as far as getting good interviews. 'A zoo

is a horrendous place to record,' says David Sproxton. 'There's so much noise going on, the acoustics are bad, the public don't like being sprung on, and the zoo authorities were getting a bit iffy.'

Ask cameraman and director of photography Andy MacCormack (or Andy Mack, as everyone at Aardman calls him) about the origins of *Creature Comforts* and he says, 'It was one of five films which were put together as a series called *Lip Synch* for Channel 4. And although they were a series, it was planned that the five films were going to be directed by five different directors. In fact, in the end Pete Lord did two of them, and the other three directors were Nick Park, Golly [Richard Goleszowski] and Bazzer [Barry Purves]. The concept behind them was based on *Conversation Pieces*, which had interviews with ordinary people, so you don't get any of that pestering stuff where people talk over each other all the time.'

The proposal for *Lip Synch* was taken to Channel 4, who had already commissioned and shown some of Aardman's previous work. As far as Nick Park was concerned, his film was probably the worst of the bunch. 'We presented them all, and mine was the least successful. I couldn't storyboard it because I didn't have the interviews, so I just did some rough sketches and interviewed some friends to see what the

> *'Trying to do as much as possible with as little as possible, that was the challenge. I think more creative things come out of that, rather than having the whole world at your disposal.'*
>
> **Nick Park**

interviews would be like, and they were all a bit dull. So mine was the one tacked on the end. And I thought it would be very much in the shadow of what Pete and Dave had already done, because it was a similar idea. I didn't think the fact that I was using animals would particularly stand out.'

The actual pitching session was a bit of a nightmare for Nick. 'I remember presenting it to the commissioning editor at Channel 4, and he hardly looked at it. It was just part of the package.'

'The way I remember it,' says Peter Lord, 'is that Nick's idea was close to what we'd done before – he'd go into the zoo and eavesdrop on people outside the cages and get them talking about the animals within. The plan would be he'd go to the monkey cage and hear people say, "Look at that very fat one there," and "What's the little one doing, mum?," and "Doesn't he look intelligent?", that kind of thing. And then he'd put those remarks into the mouths of the animals looking out. Straightforward reversal. But when he went with the sound recordist they couldn't get anything; it didn't work out, nothing was said or it was garbled, and he felt suspicious hanging around outside the cages. So the next idea was to get people *talking* about animals.'

Nick's over-riding impression of that original filming process was of the technical limitations imposed by the time available. 'We couldn't have any camera moves because we couldn't afford the time to set any up,' he remembers. 'The characters couldn't even walk because we couldn't afford to put their legs on. Most of them were just head and shoulders. Even the ones with legs couldn't go anywhere because they weren't built to move. Trying to do as much as possible with as little as possible, that was the challenge. I think more creative things come out of that, rather than having the whole world at your disposal.'

Nick's first reaction when the proposal was accepted by Channel 4 was to inject the same realistic style that Peter Lord and David Sproxton had adopted in *Animated Conversations* and *Conversation Pieces*, but he soon found his natural penchant for exaggeration coming to the fore.

'I thought, this is for Channel 4, so it can't be funny – no eyes close together, no big wide mouths, not a bit like Wallace and Gromit – it's got to be more realistic, a bit more arty. But as soon as I started work, I couldn't resist it – the eyes went close together, the mouths went big, and what it showed was that you can be artistic and funny at the same time.'

Nick did most of the interviews for the original *Creature Comforts* himself. Given the time available and his own natural diffidence, he

Above and overleaf: The bush baby was one of the more realistic animals in Creature Comforts – until it took its spectacles off. Opposite: the Gorilla from *Creature Comforts*. Nick Park's thumbprints can be seen on the nostril and upper arms in particular.

'The polar bear family used to own the shop around the corner from the studio.'

Nick Park

ended up pulling in various friends and acquaintances to help. 'The polar bear family used to own the shop around the corner from the studio. I was a bit worried because we'd told everybody it was for this animated film, but at the time no-one had seen anything like it so I don't know what they were imagining. I was a bit nervous when I showed them the polar bears, but after the first couple of shots they were on the floor, laughing. It's amazing how people automatically relate to it. This family were gathered round the viewing machine going, "Look at you! Look what you're doing!"'

The film is short – surprisingly so – but still manages to squeeze in eleven speaking animals with a family of polar bears, a rodent with its brood, an armadillo, a depressive gorilla, an elderly bush baby, a pig, a terrapin, an overly exaggerated jaguar, and a bird of uncertain genus.

David Sproxton remembers the feeling he got when *Creature Comforts* first came together. 'It was a magical moment,' he recalls. 'I can remember to this day, the first piece that Nick shot was the jaguar on the log – who I think was a Brazilian student of economics – and it was real magic.'

Richard Goleszowski was also pitching to Channel 4 on the *Lip Synch* proposal. He, like Nick Park, hadn't been in Aardman that long. 'The first thing I did was make sandwiches, make tea, make props and

Below: the unfeasibly wide Polar Bear family talking about lion steaks.
Opposite: Juxtaposition is one of the key *Creature Comforts* traits – here it's the idea of slow terrapins with a running wheel in their enclosure.

bits of set,' he remembers. 'With such a small company you end up doing a bit of everything.'

Richard Goleszowski had joined Aardman some time before Nick Park, and had actually been involved with the *Conversation Pieces* project that had, indirectly, given rise to *Lip Synch*. 'I think I came in at the tail end of the first set of films they were making for Channel 4. I'd just started making props, and I remember when the film was on TV and one of the characters held up a pound note, I was thrilled because I'd made that note!'

Andy Mack, who worked as part of the camera and lighting crew on the filming, is clear about Nick's qualities as an animator and director. 'With total respect to him, he's an absolute bloody genius but he'll be five minutes late for his own funeral. He can't bring himself to let anything go because he'll want to fiddle with it a little bit more.'

Andy's clearest memories of the original *Creature Comforts* concerns what the animals were doing in the background when the main animals were talking. 'Oh God, I can remember one bit – there's a hippo or something in the background that takes a dump! It took us at least a month to persuade Nick that it was worth doing. "Oh I don't know…" he kept saying. He wanted to drop the shot and Richard kept saying, "No, use it." And it's the bit everybody remembers now.'

The jaguar from *Creature Comforts* **would prefer to be back in his home country of Brazil.**

Having recently graduated, and spent his first years at Aardman working on commercials, Nick Park was about to hit the big time in a big way. 'Suddenly I had two films finished at the same time,' he laughs, '*Creature Comforts* and *A Grand Day Out*. The funny thing was I'd worked for seven years on *A Grand Day Out*, which was my National Film and TV School graduation project. I'd constantly anticipated that being finished, but it kept getting interrupted. And suddenly there it was on Channel 4, and Wallace and Gromit kind of came in second.'

The reaction didn't particularly surprise some of the crew who had worked on *Creature Comforts*. As Andy Mack explains, they were already aware that it was special. 'We knew when we were doing something good,' he says, 'because we liked it. And that was kind of good enough for us.'

Lip Synch consisted of five short animated films, most people – including many currently working for Aardman – would be hard pressed to name the other four. That's not to say that they are inferior – they are all, in their own ways, outstanding pieces of animation. But there's

"Where I would like to live and to spend the rest of my life? In a hot country."

something special about *Creature Comforts* that lifts it above the rest. Andy Mack, for one, is very clear about the reasons why *Creature Comforts* is still remembered with such fondness.

'I remember thinking it was a brilliant idea, the concept of using ordinary people in ordinary conversation, rather than writing the script and having actors. And I remember thinking Nick's animation was just superb – he should be out on the floor animating now, he's still one of the best around here. To be honest, I am surprised that it's taken this long to get a new series off the ground.'

It's clear from talking to Nick Park, Richard Goleszowksi and Andy Mack that their pleasure is in their work, not anticipating how it will be received. Although *Creature Comforts* won Nick various awards, that's almost a side issue. When he was making it, awards were the last thing on his mind.

'If you go down to Wetherell Place now, [where we used to work], and look right up at the ceiling,' Andy Mack says, 'just by the offices there's a punch-hole where the champagne cork hit. That was when we won the BAFTA, and we all thought that that was the top of the tree. We didn't think it could get any better. BAFTA was *it*.' He shakes his head, ruefully. 'Lo and behold, four months later we won an Oscar®.'

An animator's nightmare -– which arm is going in which direction in which shot?

the Heat Electric commercials

The short duration of most TV adverts suits the kind of length which stop-motion animation often excels at. Within the thirty- to sixty-second span of most ads it's possible to set up a situation and a punchline without labouring the point. Anything over that length has to worry about plot development and character, not to mention different sets, and then things start getting complicated.

TV commercials were, therefore, an obvious market for Aardman to move into, and move into them it did. With a vengeance. Something like one hundred products have been advertised by Aardman's talents to date. Even back in the late 1980s and early 1990s it seemed as though every commercial break in an ITV or Channel 4 programme contained something that had been animated using stop-motion techniques: the Scotch video tape skeleton, Douglas the Lurpak trombonist, the Cuprinol wood man… Inventive, yes, but also ever-present (as computer graphics are now).

Given the success of *Creature Comforts*, it seemed like an obvious next step for Aardman to transfer the style of that film to their advertising work. Up to that point, the people working on the commercials had been animating either models that were meant to represent the products themselves (dancing packets of biscuits, for instance), or were making humanoid figures actively engaged with the product (Douglas, for example).

Once *Creature Comforts* was shown on Channel 4, ad agencies quickly realized that they could produce adverts quite unlike any that had been seen before. In the same way that the original short film had turned convention on its head by putting the words of ordinary people into the mouths of model animals, a similar advert could now make something entertaining out of the old concept in which satisfied customers praised the product.

It was the Heat Electric series of adverts that took the *Creature Comforts* concept into the commercial arena. Consisting of thirteen short ads, they replicated the style of the original film perfectly, even using some of the same interviewees. Nick Park once again went around the Bristol area talking to friends, acquaintances and people he'd just met, asking them specific questions about the benefits of using electricity to heat their houses. The benefits of the *vox pop* approach immediately became clear.

'I remember the way Frank the Tortoise came out with the phrase "It's easily turn-off-and-on-able,"' says Nick Park. 'It would be very hard for a copywriter to sit down and think of that line!'

Of the remaining nine adverts, three starred a family of penguins who loved their new gas hob, including one when their grandmother turned up and was suitably impressed by the new technology in the kitchen. And the penguin voices were provided by the same family who had provided the voices for the polar bears in the original *Creature Comforts*. A brightly plumaged Brazilian bird of paradise appeared in two other ads, while two more concentrated on a pair of Scottish pandas whose dishwasher had transformed their lives. There was also one with a Liverpudlian cat, and one with mother and daughter pigs with a new electric shower.

"I'm a bit of a worrier..."

Left : Frank the Tortoise in the Heat Electric commercials. Below: Frank in the new *Creature Comforts* – older but no wiser.

"It's very comfortable. Affordable. Comfortably affordable."

'When we did the TV commercials,' Peter Lord recalls, 'we all noticed that it was the simplest TV imaginable. It was so unlike what other people were doing. Other TV commercials were like Ridley Scott doing fabulous filmic things when we were using this locked-off camera which doesn't move, characters which don't move, and just relied on good material and didn't try too hard.'

Aardman had used the voices of members of the public in various films from 1978–1989 without anyone batting an eyelid, but now that they were using them in adverts on prime-time television they suddenly discovered that they had an unexpected problem, as Nick explains. 'The actors union got upset that we were not using actors. But it would have missed the whole point if we had!'

Given the time it took to animate the animals, the first adverts were being screened while the later ones were being made. This caused more problems for Nick because people were now aware of what they were being interviewed for; in the originals they weren't. 'In fact,' he laughs, 'people got wise to it. They were volunteering; they *wanted* to be in the adverts. I was amazed how many people were willing to do it, and they'd say anything you wanted so long as it was used in the ad!'

'It was the simplest TV imaginable. It was so unlike what other people were doing.'

Peter Lord

71

The gap between the first and last ads did, however, give the advertising agency and the client – the Electricity Board – a chance to modify the way that the interviews were conducted. Market research was showing that although people were very aware of the ads, they weren't entirely clear what they were meant to be advertising.

'Everybody thought that the ads were for gas!' reveals Nick. 'The Electricity Board asked us if we could get the interviewees to say "electricity" a bit more often! And people would go, "Oh, I love my new electric cooker!" The danger was that they started to sound as if they were being prompted.'

The whole point of using members of the public had been, of course, that what they said sounded spontaneous and honest. That was because it *was* spontaneous and honest. If they were in on the joke the adverts would now sound false, a problem that also occurred on the new *Creature Comforts*.

In an ironic twist, the Heat Electric adverts are probably better remembered than the original *Creature Comforts* film that spawned them. They are cosy and warm (just the kind of association that the advertising agency wanted), and there's something honest and endearing about the animals. Even Johnny Morris's voice, reading out the tag line at the end of each ad, exudes trustworthiness. The ads have recently been voted near the top of the list of the UK's favourite adverts. (They

'Everybody thought that the ads were for gas! The Electricity Board asked us if we could get the interviewees to say "electricity" a bit more often.'

Nick Park

The Heat Electric cat may have been the most realistic animal created by Aardman.

were beaten by the Guinness 'wild horses' advert, Smash – a reconstituted mashed potato mix promoted by puppet Martians, and the Tango ad with people being attacked by a large orange man in a loincloth.) Watching the Heat Electric adverts again now, and they are available on several video and DVD compilations of Aardman material, they still seem fresher and funnier than almost any other advert on TV.

Despite the huge amount of interest in the Heat Electric adverts, and the publicity surrounding their inclusion in the 100 Most Memorable Adverts list drawn up by *The Sunday Times* and Channel 4 in 2000, it's not common knowledge that while twelve adverts were made for the campaign only eleven were shown. The unseen, finished advert concerns two orang-utans discussing the washing needs of their families but it was never shown following concerns about the way the characters were portrayed.

"Brilliant what they can do with technology today."

So, is the towel made of Plasticine as well?

Part Three: The New Creature Comforts

creature comforts returns

Things have changed in the fourteen years since the original *Creature Comforts* was first shown. In 1989, Britain only had four television channels, and the one that showed *Creature Comforts* – Channel 4 – was still regarded as a new channel aimed at minority audiences. Now, as the revived version of *Creature Comforts* makes its debut, it's possible to flick through hundreds of different channels, many of them aimed deliberately at audiences far smaller in number than Channel 4 ever managed on its worst days.

And tastes have changed, too. Computer-generated imagery means that children's animation can now be produced to a standard that was, in 1989, only achievable in hugely budgeted Hollywood movies. Programmes are edited to run at a frantic pace so as not to bore a generation raised on computer games, and odd camera angles abound in order to catch the roving eye.

Some things, however, still remain the same. People *still* like the idea of Plasticine models and love slower paced programmes without obvious jokes, teen slang or garish MTV colours. So perhaps the difference is not between an old style and a new style, but between a new and a classic style that always remains in vogue despite the passing fashions that flash and fade around it. And *Creature Comforts* definitely sits in the classic group.

A quick search on the UK's premier internet auction site Ebay, tapping in the phrase 'Creature Comforts', shows that people are still trading in plush toys based on the characters, even after all this time, with Frank the Tortoise being a perennial favourite. The characters appear to have lodged in the collective consciousness of the UK population whereas other characters from longer, flashier and more expensive programmes have faded into obscurity, banished to that little section of limbo reserved for memories that nobody bothers to remember any more.

A great deal has been written over the years about the British character. Great minds and well-known pundits have attempted to analyse exactly what it is that separates us from our European neighbours on one side and our transatlantic cousins on the other. What makes us, forms us, defines us? Perhaps the answer lies in a tortoise with a bizarrely

> "I don't think I've got any other scars, not physical ones, mental ones obviously. I've got a lot of them but you can't see them because they're inside my brain."
>
> **Fluffy the hamster**

Angus H. Wintergreen is a consummate performer, an elephant whose life has been inextricably bound up with the circus since he was born.

The thing that excites Angus the most about performing is that there's a release of any tensions he might have inside of him. He strongly believes that a performer has to communicate with the audience but mustn't look at them because the performer is apart from them and it would break the illusion.

Angus frequently feels sick before a performance, but is convinced that if there aren't a few butterflies around, in the tummy, before he goes on stage then he's probably not going to give a good performance.

A possible move from the circus ring to television isn't something that Angus had really considered, but he wouldn't be averse to trying if the chance came. It would, he feels, be a new dimension.

"It's a release of any tensions that you might have inside you..."

angus h. wintergreen

wide mouth and a family of bickering polar bears. Perhaps the fact that these characters are still recognizable, still popular and still important tells us something about what the British care about. Animals, for a start – we certainly care about animals. And we're big on irony, and what we hear in *Creature Comforts* is certainly completely at odds with what we see. And, of course, we love the endearing amateurishness of it all. Not to take anything away from the sheer hard work and talent of Nick Park and the rest of the people at Aardman, but *Creature Comforts* has the feel of something lovingly crafted by artisans and not assembled by production-line technicians.

The period between the original *Creature Comforts* and the new one has also seen many changes for Aardman Animations. In 1989 it was small enough for all the employees to fit in a single room. Now they inhabit three separate sites, and the plaque outside the main company premises lists nine different companies under the Aardman umbrella. It has gone from being a small, specialist supplier of short animated features to a company producing movies that can attract the voices of major Hollywood stars, and which can compete in the cut-throat international market.

This page and opposite: As much effort is put into making background props as the creatures themselves.

The decision to return to *Creature Comforts* couldn't have been easy. There's always been the desire to move on, to make something bigger and better. Each of the short Wallace and Gromit films, for instance, was more ambitious than the last, and *Chicken Run* was a leap into new territory. Perhaps it was the postponement of the second movie project, *Tortoise and Hare* (a subject that the staff at Aardman Features still find too sensitive to talk about) that provoked them to fall back on something familiar. Perhaps they felt they were deviating too far from their roots.

One of the many strengths of Aardman is the way that the company's founders give new talent the opportunity to flourish. A constant theme, during the research for this book, was the way that animators and model-makers had been brought in, often part-time or as apprentices, and encouraged to develop their talents and discover what they are good at. Just as Nick Park was given the chance to finish his own project when he joined Aardman – a project that became the Wallace and Gromit piece, *A Grand Day Out* – so a half-dozen animators were given a chance, after they had finished working on *Chicken Run*, to make their own, one-minute pieces. It's a necessary but courageous piece of company thinking – after all, the *next* Nick Park has to come from somewhere.

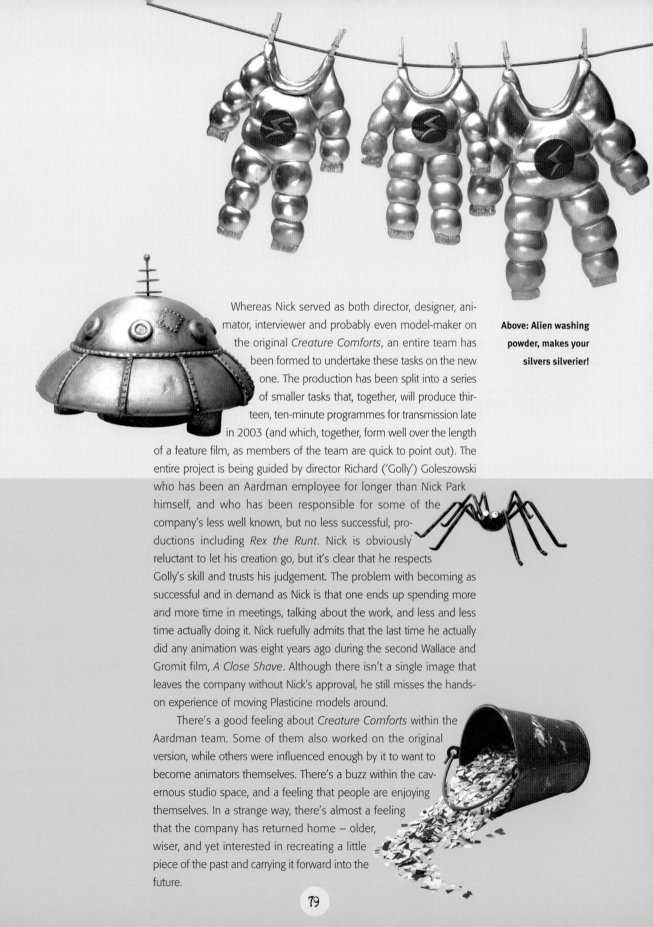

Whereas Nick served as both director, designer, animator, interviewer and probably even model-maker on the original *Creature Comforts*, an entire team has been formed to undertake these tasks on the new one. The production has been split into a series of smaller tasks that, together, will produce thirteen, ten-minute programmes for transmission late in 2003 (and which, together, form well over the length of a feature film, as members of the team are quick to point out). The entire project is being guided by director Richard ('Golly') Goleszowski who has been an Aardman employee for longer than Nick Park himself, and who has been responsible for some of the company's less well known, but no less successful, productions including *Rex the Runt*. Nick is obviously reluctant to let his creation go, but it's clear that he respects Golly's skill and trusts his judgement. The problem with becoming as successful and in demand as Nick is that one ends up spending more and more time in meetings, talking about the work, and less and less time actually doing it. Nick ruefully admits that the last time he actually did any animation was eight years ago during the second Wallace and Gromit film, *A Close Shave*. Although there isn't a single image that leaves the company without Nick's approval, he still misses the hands-on experience of moving Plasticine models around.

There's a good feeling about *Creature Comforts* within the Aardman team. Some of them also worked on the original version, while others were influenced enough by it to want to become animators themselves. There's a buzz within the cavernous studio space, and a feeling that people are enjoying themselves. In a strange way, there's almost a feeling that the company has returned home – older, wiser, and yet interested in recreating a little piece of the past and carrying it forward into the future.

Above: Alien washing powder, makes your silvers silverier!

commissioning & creating

It seems obvious now that the new *Creature Comforts* would be almost guaranteed a good reception from TV audiences, but it took the people at Aardman a long time to be convinced. 'It had often been suggested in the past,' recalls Aardman co-founder Peter Lord. 'In fact when we made the first *Creature Comforts*, the American TV stations who love mass production, were saying, "Oh give us one hundred and fifty of those, that'd be great." But we reckoned, no, it can't be done. You can't mass produce it. Then, when the idea was raised again in 2002, there was a general consensus that it was the right time to go for it.

'I don't know exactly how it happened,' says Peter, 'but when it did it was like a great relief. And we thought, yes, it's so obvious. It was like answering a question that had been asked fifteen years ago.'

'I came up with the idea for the new series,' explains Nick Park, who directed the original *Creature Comforts*. 'And I came up with about twelve or thirteen episode ideas, with a brief synopsis of how they might go. We asked Golly to direct them, and I chatted to him at length about them all: he was interested in doing it and I thought he was the best person for the job. He was around when we did the original, and I felt he understood it. He understood where it was coming from, and I've always appreciated his own humour in *Rex the Runt* and *Robbie the Reindeer*.'

Golly is aware of how fortunate he is to be handling the new *Creature Comforts*. 'I think Nick always wanted to do it,' he says, 'because of all its possibilities, but it always took a back burner because of his feature projects and other commitments. I think he's quite jealous that I'm directing it!'

And it didn't take long for Golly to be aware that Aardman had a winner on its hands. 'Once we started to explore the series, it was a real revelation how fantastic it could be when you start recording people's voices and you hear what they say. It was incredible, it felt like a really rich, fertile area had suddenly opened up.'

Peter Lord and David Sproxton considered various TV stations, but they quickly decided to approach ITV with the proposal for the series. The world of television is different now to when the first *Creature Comforts* was put together – animation is now a mainstream genre, and Aardman has more than proved its credentials.

ITV jumped at the chance to transmit something that was as close to a guaranteed hit as it was possible to get, and Aardman started building up a team to put the series together. With Golly on board as director and Nick roughing out some initial character sketches, studio space was booked and the whole panoply of designers, model makers and animators began to assemble…

"I think the standard of British food, I think is first class, it, somehow clean, umm, satisfying."
Constantine II

the producer's role

Julie Lockhart solves one of the many problems that crop up during the course of a working day. Are those apples real or Plasticine? It's difficult to tell at Aardman.

Most of the people who have worked on *Creature Comforts* have been involved with a single aspect – the model-making, the lighting, the music and so on. Julie Lockhart, however, is the show's producer, which means that she has been involved from beginning to end, controlling every aspect of the entire production.

'I'm responsible for everything,' Julie explains. 'My role is to make sure that the production runs smoothly and there's enough scope creatively for the director to do what he wants to do, within the boundaries of a certain budget and a certain schedule which has been agreed with Aardman and with ITV. If the director says he's never been pressured budget- or schedule-wise then I've done my job.'

One of Julie's first jobs within Aardman was working with Nick Park on the original *Heat Electric* commercials, the ones based on the style of the original *Creature Comforts* short film. Following the success of the *Heat Electric* campaign she worked on many more commercials, and ended up running the entire Aardman commercials department. A move to the broadcast side of the company came next, with Julie producing the first series of *Angry Kid*, before becoming involved with developing new shows for Aardman.

Although it was obvious that the new *Creature Comforts* had to be similar in look and style to the original, it's not easy to expand from what was a five minute film on one theme to a hundred and thirty minutes on thirteen different themes. 'Because the original film was such a valuable property for Aardman,' Julie says, 'and because it was so charming, we wanted to do it justice. We were very tentative about making sure that we'd got the right length, and that we had enough material for people to talk about. Now, of course, we know that we could have had hundreds of themes and recorded hundreds and hundreds of people and we wouldn't have had any problem.'

> 'I'm responsible for everything. My role is to make sure that the production runs smoothly and there's enough scope creatively for the director.'
> **Julie Lockhart**

From beginning to end, *Creature Comforts* has taken about eighteen months to make, and Julie's been there every step of the way. 'Aardman started developing the project over Christmas 2001,' she explains. 'Then the development had a break for a couple of months while funding was raised, and luckily there wasn't any problem with that. We started the production for real in April 2002 and spent six months interviewing, recording and getting our heads around the project before we started shooting in September 2002.'

The critical first step was to think up the themes for the episodes. 'Four or five of us would sit in a room,' Julie recalls, 'and we'd think of an episode and we'd think, 'who do we want to interview? What type of person? What sorts of things do we want them to say?' We'd then write questions for each episode. It's hugely important how you phrase the questions, because they need to be answered in a way that you could imagine an animal answering them.'

One of the techniques was to provoke answers that could be used in a variety of contexts: 'Wanting to get people emotive about something, and then using that emotion for a different visual gag,' Julie remembers. 'So we might ask "do you feel stressed?" and they would go, "Yeah, I always feel under pressure!" and we could use that anywhere – a mole in the garden, a fish deep under water, whatever…'

'Who do we want to interview? What type of person? What sorts of things do we want them to say?'
Julie Lockhart

The interviewing process was the cornerstone of the entire project. In order to make Creature Comforts work, Aardman needed a large number of people to say fascinating things in a variety of accents. And that's not the kind of thing you can just arrange in a day or two.

'We had an idea that we'd be able to record, edit everything and then just shoot it,' Julie says, 'but what happened was that, after the first batch or recording, we might have had twenty per cent of the first batch of episodes finished, and after the second batch of recording we might have had thirty per cent. Gradually we'd be building up and building up, while still leaving it creatively very open, so that, even ten months into the shooting, if we'd found someone with fantastic views on the garden, for instance, then there was still an opening to record them and slot them in.'

This open-ended, organic way of working meant, of course, that Julie as producer and Golly as director had to be able to focus on all the different aspects of the production together rather than sequentially. 'We're recording, editing, building the models, designing the sets, building the sets, shooting, animating, editing, doing post production, all at the same time,' says Julie. 'Much respect is due to Golly, because at any one point he's been having to answer questions on the very first bits of pre-production through to post-production, and all of the things in-between, because they've all been going on simultaneously.'

Sady, some of the people who were interviewed will not hear their voices coming out of the mouth of a Plasticine animal. That's just the way the process works – some of the material gets cut out along the way. Julie, however, is ecstatic about the success rate that they have achieved. 'We've interviewed three hundred and fifty people,' she says, 'and we've got about a hundred and fifty characters, which is nearly a one in two hit rate. A lot of that is down to good questioning. A lot of credit should go to the interviewers – they would go and find interesting people and interview them in such a way that we could use the material.'

And, of course, the quirky characteristics of the Great British Public helped.

'If the public weren't talking naturally then we wouldn't have been able to make the series,' Julie agrees. 'You can easily tell if someone's performing.'

With so much going on in the production, it's sometimes difficult to tell what outsiders might make of it all. Julie remembers one moment in particular that jolted her back to reality for a moment.

'One of the first characters we built was a big, pink, phallic worm,' she laughs, 'and there was one day, when we were showing people round the studio, we came to the worm and I suddenly though, 'Oh my God, what kind of impression are we making here?'

Dave the Worm, one of the simplest characters to build and animate, but one of the most memorable.

'If the public weren't talking naturally then we wouldn't have been able to make the series. You can easily tell if someone's performing.'

Julie Lockhart

episode themes

Working Animals

How does a cockroach multi-task? Where does an owl go to find clerical work? How do guard dogs cope when their timetables are re-arranged, and why do lab rats fear retirement? Find out what our animal friends really think about life under the hand of man.

The original *Creature Comforts* lasted for five minutes, and had a group of animals in a zoo talking mainly about the terms of their captivity. The new *Creature Comforts* series lasts in total for just over two hours, and it doesn't take the brains of an archbishop to work out that the monologues would have to cover a lot more ground for the series to maintain audience interest.

Nick Park and Richard Goleszowski decided that each episode should tackle a different theme, and that the themes should, where possible, reflect common concerns with the audience. They should be the kind of topics that might spring up in the pub or at a bus stop. And they had to provoke those being inter-viewed to react strongly and talk at length, so that the Aardman team could pick and choose from plenty of recorded material. The themes should also provoke vivid memories and anecdotes.

When Golly started planning *Creature Comforts* he was concerned that it should work as a series, and that the episodes shouldn't just show a collection of animals talking. Each one had to be a documentary. 'And don't forget that the episodes are twice as long as the original,' he says, 'so you can't get away with just gags, there has to be some kind of narrative and documentary structure that'll draw you in. Eight minutes of talking heads isn't good enough.'

After a lot of head scratching and dis-cussion, thirteen themes were chosen. Interviewers were chosen, tape recorders dispatched and instructions issued. At selected locations around the UK people were either ambushed in their homes or stopped on the street and asked how they felt about a whole range of subjects. And, as the tapes began to roll, they began to talk…

The Sea

What does a shark do when it's scared of the deep? How does a plankton ride with waves? Can a shrimp hold its breath longer than a jellyfish, and what happens when a walrus gets the bends?...Swimming lessons from the experts.

The Beach

What do starfish think of noise pollution? Can an octopus eat ice creams in a strong wind? Do sea anenomes enjoy sharing their pool with strangers, and why do sea lions prefer Whitby to Scarborough? Pull up a deckchair, don the kiss me quick, and let our coastal creatures soothe away the winter blues.

Feeding Time

How does an arthritic seagull get into a bag of crisps? What do oysters do to a bloodhound's brain? Is pet food as tasty as it looks, and if a pigeon ate chicken, would that make it a cannibal? Peel back the lid to discover who visited your dustbin last night.

What's It All About ?

What came first, the diplodocus, or the sparrow? Did slugs emerge from volcanos, and how does a domestic cat feel about crawling from the primordial ooze? Join a grab bag of nature's finest as they try to work out where they came from.

86

The Garden

Why don't worms like fresh air? Where does a woodpecker go for contemplation? What do slugs think about organic gardening, and when does a pond become a singles bar for frogs? All is revealed when the garden dwellers discuss life in their urban turf.

Being A Bird

What makes a bird stay in the air? How does the homing instinct work, and what happens when a pigeon falls through a skylight? All this and more, as our feathered friends reveal the ups and downs of life in the sky.

Cats or Dogs?

What do dogs think about Crufts? Do cats like cuddles, and who makes the better burglar alarm? Take a ringside seat as the two most popular pets go head to head in a battle that's raged for centuries.

'Merry Christmas'

Why does a guide dog pursue a caretaker, and what do reindeer think of Santa? Why do hamsters dread chemistry sets, and what do mice think of mince pies? Christmas is for all animals not just for dogs!

The Pet Shop

Are squeaky toys degrading to dogs? How much does a goldfish think its worth? Do chameleons suffer from self image problems, and why do stick insects make better conversationalists than spaniels? Potential pets face their fear of being left on the shelf.

The Circus

Have you ever wondered what it's like to be fired out of a canon? Or how an elephant combats stage fright, or a performing seal masters the art of the French horn? Well, here's your chance to find out, as a motley crew of circus animals lift the lid on life under the big top.

Is Anyone Out There?

Who are the little green men and why do they want to holiday here? Take a journey into the unexpected, as our interstellar friends wrestle with postman etiquette, and the weather.

Pets at the Vets

A Piranha with toothache, a pig with sunstroke, a performing dog with an aversion to feet, and a monkey who loves intrusive injections...Take a peek behind the surgery door, as under the weather pets vent spleen in the waiting room.

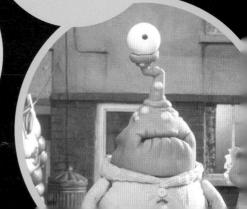

directing

If there is ever a reunion of the people who worked on the original *Creature Comforts*, they'll all fit quite comfortably in a small van. The new version, by contrast, is being made by so many people that a double decker bus would be required. And the man charged with controlling all these disparate creative personalities is director Richard Goleszowski.

'I was Aardman's first employee, I think,' he recalls. 'Aardman was a two-man company at the time with just Peter Lord and David Sproxton, and they got me in to build some sets and models. I arrived at the end of the first set of the *Animated Conversations* films they were making for Channel 4, and stayed for nine years!'

Golly then left Aardman to set up on his own, but returned on a number of occasions to work on programmes such as *Rex the Runt*. When he was offered the chance to take charge of *Creature Comforts* he jumped at it, although he was well aware of the scale of the task.

'Remember,' he says, 'that the original *Creature Comforts* was just five minutes long, and took three months to make. The new episodes are twice as long as the original so we are, in one year, producing twenty-six times the original amount. The increased scale is matched by an

It's amazing, what lies beneath an ordinary suburban house... In fact, the set for the aliens' house is built on a platform inside a soundstage. The 'sky' is a painted backdrop.

> **'I was Aardman's first employee... it was a two-man company at the time with just Peter Lord and Dave Sproxton, and they got me in to build some sets and models.'**
> Richard Goleszowski

increase in the number
of characters that need to be
animated. 'I think it's going to be somewhere
around one hundred and twenty,' he says. 'But the thing to remember
about *Creature Comforts* is that it's not a drama, it's a mock-documentary. That's why there are so many characters.'

Golly knew from the start that as director he had to be involved in
all the creative decisions, from the choice of episode themes to the
recording of the interviews, the character designs and the animation. His
fingerprints are on every aspect of the show.

**Richard 'Golly'
Goleszowski has
directed every episode
of the new *Creature
Comforts*.**

Above: Sid and Nancy's garden shed, prepared for filming, awaits the arrival of its two inhabitants. Opposite: Sid and Nancy relax while awaiting their cue.

'I couldn't just come in and direct somebody else's script and storyboard,' he points out. 'Then it becomes just a mechanical process. It's very hard to be a jobbing director in model animation because it's such a long process – you're going to get bored if it's not your idea, and you're not going to have the same commitment if you haven't got an involvement in the story telling and writing.'

One of the early decisions, one that makes the process easier to manage, as well as giving the show a crisp, clean look, was to abandon the traditional film cameras used in stop-motion animation. 'We're not using any film at all, which is fantastic,' Golly adds. 'It's all shot digitally, goes into a computer and then gets transferred to the editing room. That cuts out so many headaches, and it looks great.'

'They've all got particular strengths that you play to, so you give them characters you think they'll work well with and be inspired by.'
Golly

The making of any film or television process can roughly be divided into three separate areas, pre-production, production and post-production. Pre-production on *Creature Comforts* involves choosing the themes for the individual episodes, recording members of the public, choosing the best lines from the interviews, designing the creatures and building the world they inhabit. Post-production involves editing the final material into a coherent structure. Sandwiched in the middle is the production phase. Normally, with live action, that would involve telling actors where to move and what to do. Here, it's much the same, except you get middle-men. Golly is directing the animators, explaining how he wants the Plasticine creatures to move, and they have to interpret his directions in their own particular ways. One of his main concerns is the need for the episodes to have a consistent style while allowing the animators some freedom of expression.

'The animators are very talented,' he explains, 'and they've all got particular strengths that you play to, so you give them characters you think they'll work well with and be inspired by. They work very differently. Some work really quickly, and some quite slowly and are very considered. You can't issue a blanket request for everyone to do a certain amount of work each day; you've just got to try and get them to work as hard as possible!'

Having so many different animators makes it difficult to predict how much usable material each animator will produce by the end of each day. Although it would be nice to think of Aardman Animations as some kind of small craft workshop, it's actually a business. And, like all businesses, it has deadlines to meet.

'The animators' output can vary from two seconds a day – which is actually the speed that *Chicken Run* was shot at – to eight or ten seconds a day,' says Golly. 'That gives us an average of around four to five seconds a day, which is actually what we're trying to hit, thank goodness!'

'It's not a drama, it's a mock-documentary. That's why there are so many characters.'
Golly

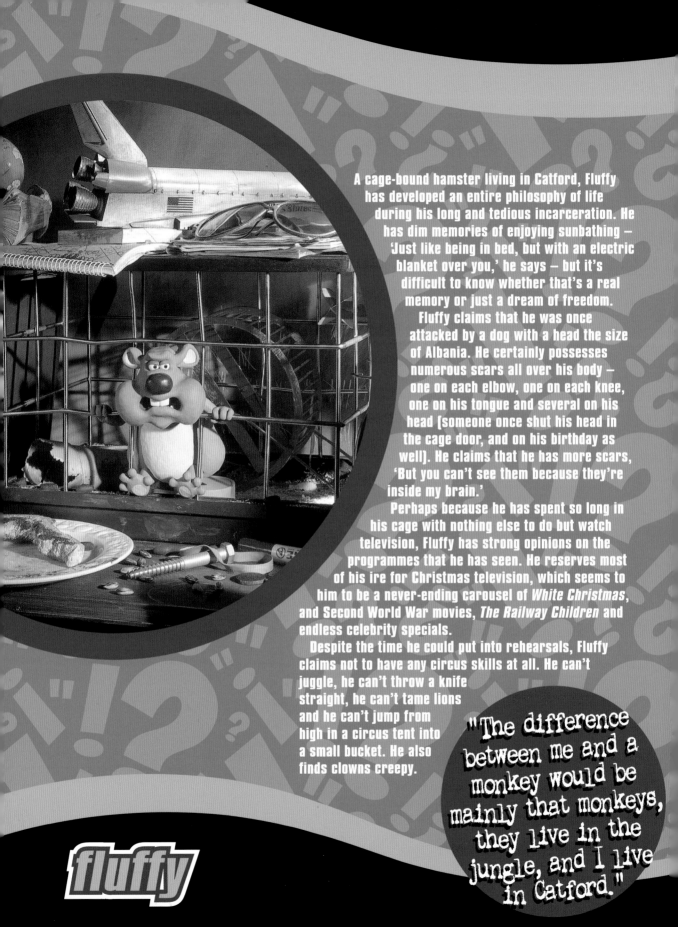

A cage-bound hamster living in Catford, Fluffy has developed an entire philosophy of life during his long and tedious incarceration. He has dim memories of enjoying sunbathing – 'Just like being in bed, but with an electric blanket over you,' he says – but it's difficult to know whether that's a real memory or just a dream of freedom. Fluffy claims that he was once attacked by a dog with a head the size of Albania. He certainly possesses numerous scars all over his body – one on each elbow, one on each knee, one on his tongue and several on his head (someone once shut his head in the cage door, and on his birthday as well). He claims that he has more scars, 'But you can't see them because they're inside my brain.'

Perhaps because he has spent so long in his cage with nothing else to do but watch television, Fluffy has strong opinions on the programmes that he has seen. He reserves most of his ire for Christmas television, which seems to him to be a never-ending carousel of *White Christmas*, and Second World War movies, *The Railway Children* and endless celebrity specials.

Despite the time he could put into rehearsals, Fluffy claims not to have any circus skills at all. He can't juggle, he can't throw a knife straight, he can't tame lions and he can't jump from high in a circus tent into a small bucket. He also finds clowns creepy.

"The difference between me and a monkey would be mainly that monkeys, they live in the jungle, and I live in Catford."

fluffy

recording the voices

The things the animals say in *Creature Comforts* sound unscripted and unrehearsed, but each episode is the result of a painstaking process of winnowing down thousands of hours of interviews until what remains is pure, dramatic gold.

Toby Farrow is one of the team responsible for looking after the tapes and assembling them into thirteen coherent narratives. Although he has only undertaken a few of the interviews himself, he has listened to them all many times. And nobody knows better than he how many interviews have been recorded.

'At the last count it was something like two hundred and seventy,' he sighs. 'It's a huge amount. Nick, I think, did about sixty interviews for the original *Creature Comforts* for just a small number of characters – I think it was about seven or eight in the original. That's a hit rate of five, but ours has been about one in two.'

'We use approximately 50 per cent of the voices that we record,' adds Golly, 'which is a very, very high ratio compared with what we were expecting. We thought we'd use an awful lot less than that. But *Creature Comforts* gives you the scope for developing characters over the episode, and it also gives you the scope for adding one-liners. It's inevitable that in a ninety-minute interview, no matter how dull it is, you'll find one good line for one particular animal.'

Golly was originally involved in conducting the interviews, but as time went on and the scale of the process became apparent, he took more of a back seat. According to Toby Farrow, 'We've got a network of people around the UK, and their job is to find interesting people. We've started to use radio interviewers a lot more now because they've got such a wealth of good people to interview, and their technique is very good.'

'What you find inevitably,' says David Sproxton, one of the show's executive producers, 'is that a lot of the material you recorded early on you begin to strip out, because better stuff comes through as time goes on, you've learned better interviewing techniques, you may have found better interviewers, you've certainly found better interviewees, and you've also found the angle you want.'

Toby Farrow in his usual pose – headphones on, listening to yet another interview. Behind him are stacked some of the many CDs that hold completed interviews.

'We've got a network of people around the UK, and their job is to find interesting people.'

Toby Farrow

93

Some of the interviews were conducted in the street, or in locations such as doctors' surgeries and vets' waiting rooms. Others took place in people's homes. Toby found that some of the best interviews occurred in places with a strong sense of location. 'We interviewed people on the beach,' he recalls, 'and, because it's got such a strong atmosphere, because they can actually see the waves and the pebbles, it helps their words come alive.'

Toby's experience is that people are quite happy to be interviewed, for the most part. More than happy, sometimes. 'I think as soon as you put a microphone in somebody's face it's almost like they have a yearning to tell you about themselves in a way that they never do in real life. We've had quite a lot of reticent people and you think, oh, we're never going to get any information out of you, but the strange thing with the microphone is that people just start confessing. Sometimes you want to shout, "Stop it!" because it's actually going to be heard by millions of people.'

'It's a bit like therapy, I suppose,' David Sproxton muses.

Everyone who takes part knows that their words might be put into the mouths of Plasticine creatures, but they are encouraged to talk as honestly as they can. That's one of the key strengths of *Creature Comforts* – the creatures are animals who don't think they're animals. Frank the Tortoise, for instance, doesn't give any impression that he thinks he's a tortoise. And this can lead to problems, as Toby explains. 'Sometimes somebody guesses which animal their voice might be used for. And then it all goes pear-shaped because they become too knowing and lose any innocence.. They try and play it up and give you what they think you want. But actually what you want is for them to be completely oblivious to what they are.'

Golly agrees. 'When we started we thought that the best thing would be to find good raconteurs. And we found one chap in Yorkshire who is a terrific talker; in fact that's what he did for a living, he did

'**The strange thing with the microphone is that people just start confessing. Sometimes you want to shout, "Stop it!"'**
Toby Farrow

Those people who thought it was a real interviewer's hand in shot are in for a surprise!

guided tours of York and he's a really good racon-teur, but because every single sentence was perfectly enunciated, he sounded trained, and that doesn't work: there has to be that hesitancy and awkwardness of real conversation.'

The actual process of con-ducting the interviews has changed over the course of time. 'When we started the project it was very random,' Toby explains. 'Anybody that we thought might be inter-esting, we interviewed, but as it's gone on we've become much more selective. Particularly in the later episodes we've started to target people who we think we can actually use. We've tried to think of the gags that we'd like to use, and then we try to find people who might be able to deliver them. For example, we've got a paranoid snake stuck in a pet shop; but what are its fears? So we went and interviewed a guy who'd been stuck in a lift.'

A similar process occurs in building up the episodes from so many disparate elements. 'Maybe we'll think, oh, we need a funny bit here, so we go and interview twenty people in the hope that we can get that one line. It's a real trial and error process, and you just can't predict what you're going to get.'

Once the interviews are complete and Toby has the transcripts in front of him, he starts the painstaking process of going through them looking for lines to use. And he's also trying to get some idea, some image of the characters behind the voices.

'Generally,' he explains, 'what you do is look for a little clue as to character. It might be just one word, or a particular phrase. Then, after you've read the transcript and heard the tape three or four times, the character starts to emerge. It's a really strange process. Sometimes we'll do it the other way round, and create the character or screen image first and then add a voice, but it works best if the voice determines the character. And once you add the right image, it all clicks. Of course, sometimes the process doesn't work and you'll get six transcripts where you can't think of any character at all.'

'If you can avoid meeting the interviewees you simply have no idea what they look like,' David Sproxton explains, 'and everything you create

Toby Farrow works on more interview transcriptions.

'We found one chap in Yorkshire who is a terrific talker, in fact that's what he did for a living; he's a really good raconteur.'
Golly

for them comes purely from the voice. Sometimes you can have surprises when you meet them later on.'

A large part of the pleasure in creating the characters lies in contrasting what they say – or their tone of voice – with the look of the creature that's actually mouthing the words. 'If somebody's being quite pompous,' Toby admits, 'then it's quite fun to give them a small, insignificant character, and if they're very shy then you can make them into something big, like a tiger.'

The couple whose voices eventually became a laid back cat and dog were a good example where what was being said contrasted with how it was being said. 'They're a classic case,' agrees Toby. 'They're very, very close, get on with each other very well, and I think have really good repartee. One of them hates cats, the other hates dogs, and when they're talking it's perfectly natural, but of course if you turn them into the cat and the dog you suddenly bring it all to life.'

Sometimes, there's a conversational subtext which flies up to the surface. 'We've got a couple of characters that we've made into rats', Golly explains, 'and sadly they've actually split up since the interview, but you could sense that tension when they talked to each other. And I don't know if it's unfortunate or fortunate, but that gives you strong material: you can sense that there's a problem.'

Of course, there's a fine line in the making of the episodes between humour and cruelty. It would be all too easy to make the people giving the interviews sound stupid. Nick Park is well aware of the risks. 'I think

'If somebody's being quite pompous, then it's quite fun to give them a small, insignificant character.'
Toby Farrow

Below: Golly holds one of his regular meetings with the team. Behind him, character sketches line the walls.

Above and below:
Cindy Jones,
pre-production
co-ordinator, and
her dog, Dax.

there is a dignity question,' he says, 'especially with some of the older people that were interviewed. You could easily have them doing something obscene in the background and get a laugh from some of the students, but you've got to be careful. People in interviews are vulnerable, especially if they're not that aware of the medium and how you can use it. You can easily manipulate people and get them to come across just as you want by straightforward editing.'

'I think one of Nick's philosophies is that the person doing the talking is not made to look foolish,' Toby adds. 'You can have the background characters doing stupid things, but the actual character being interviewed is treated very seriously. I think people know that they're not going to get stitched up.'

Some of the interviewees are so good that they come back time and time again. And sometimes, even though the animators don't get to see what the interviewees look like, odd coincidences can happen. Take, for example, the dog and the cat. 'We interviewed them about four or five times,' Toby recalls. 'We showed them their animations after their last interview but it was really weird because, totally by chance, the guy who was playing the cat was sitting on the sofa in exactly the same pose!'

creating the characters

A fastidious lioness who doesn't like clowns, a plankton with a philosophical bent… These are some of the bizarre characters that *Creature Comforts* will be best remembered for.

The chain of events that leads from someone being interviewed on the street or beach, to their words coming out of the mouth of an animal or alien creature, is long and not particularly straightforward. All kinds of factors influence the decision as to what creatures to match against what voices. And often the decision is driven by the pictures conjured up in the heads of the people at Aardman when they hear the tapes.

'Sometimes a voice sounds like a particular character, and sometimes the character is derived from what is said,' Golly confides. 'For instance, we had somebody who was interrupted by his mother during the interview and said, "Oh, you've got a problem, mother? Can you get back in your little hole?" and we thought that's perfect, we'll make him a worm'.

Another character who sprang to life the moment the tape was played was the hamster in the cage. 'We interviewed a chap who sounds like he's slightly lonely and down,' says Golly. 'He's got a very dry sense of humour. And we just thought he'd be perfect for a hamster that belongs to somebody who's just outgrown it. So we've got the pet in a cage in a teenager's bedroom with posters on the wall, and the hamster's become a bit of the furniture. To show this we've got darts that have been thrown through the cage and hit the back wall. So the hamster's become slightly superfluous to needs, and his voice is perfect for that.'

"It's just pants – I don't believe in it."
Dave the Worm

'We had somebody who was interrupted by his mother during the interview and said, "Oh, you've got a problem, mother? Can you get back in your little hole?"'
Golly

"Whelks, mussels ... that's like eating slugs ... sliding down your gullet ... "

Trixie and Captain Cuddlepuss are primarily sofa inhabitants who find their domestic arrangements entirely satisfactory. They seem to spend most of their lives on the sofa, with Captain Cuddlepuss sprawled out comfortably, pontificating on the state of the world, and Trixie demurely perched on a corner interjecting with her own opinions every now and then.

Captain Cuddlepuss has a penchant for fresh chicken served on a hand-painted Chinese saucer, whereas Trixie enjoys nothing more than a brisk constitutional around the local civic ground (despite the ever-present hazards of dog-mess).

Captain Cuddlepuss has been chased by a great Dane, been bitten by a beagle and pursued by an old English sheepdog, but he loves kittens, he thinks they're brilliant.

trixie & captain cuddlepuss

"You can't be morbid."
Norman the Maggot

The original character design for Norman the Maggot.

'The cat is a chap who's quite slow and dry, but when we interviewed him I was aware that he was actually rather nervous.'
Golly

Other animals are realized more as a reaction against the sound of the voice, in an attempt to produce some kind of creative tension. 'Take the cat and the dog on the sofa,' Golly adds. 'The cat is a chap whose delivery is quite slow and dry, but when we interviewed him I was aware that he was actually rather nervous; he'd sit with his hands between his knees, slightly hunched, and when I asked him a question he'd always check for his partner's approval. He was actually quite self-effacing and spoke so slowly, but we subverted him into quite an arrogant character. I hope that people won't think that he really is like that, because he isn't.'

The cat and dog are probably the characters who appear most in *Creature Comforts*. 'They've got an opinion on everything, and they're incredibly dry and very funny,' says Golly. Other characters just appear for the sake of a quick joke and vanish again. Golly adds, 'We've got a maggot in one shot, who is being lowered through the frame. You don't realize what's going on, you just see an image of a riverbank, and this maggot comes past on a hook. (It's sat on the hook, by the way, not speared by it.) And he says, "Well, you have to laugh, don't you? It's either you or them, really, isn't' it?" and he just disappears out of frame again.'

And, the good news for fans of the original *Creature Comforts*, is that some of the original interviewees are back again…

'In the original Creature Comforts there's a family of polar bears,' recalls Golly, 'and the interviewees were actually a family with two young sons, now in their twenties. And from what they said it seemed appropriate to make them sea anemones – if you watch the series you'll find out why.'

Although the decision as to which voice goes with which character is key to what appears on screen, there are other decisions to make. One is how to present the characters. Take, for instance, the elderly man who, when interviewed, talked a lot about his experiences with doctors and hospitals. Golly decided early on to make him a rather woebegone bloodhound.

'I knew a bloodhound that used to make people laugh because of its heavy and really worried brow,' Golly says. 'If you laughed it would just raise its eyebrows and look at you, and then drop them again when you stopped, and raise them if you made another noise. And that look seemed to work perfectly for our bloodhound.'

The decision was then how exactly to present him on camera. 'Because the way he talks is almost confessional,' Golly reveals, 'I thought we'd show him in profile: almost in silhouette, like people who don't really want to be identified on TV. I thought that seemed appropriate. But it's not very helpful when developing a charac-ter if you just see it in profile, so I thought well, if he's downtrodden, you kind of want to see him sat on the floor, as if the camera was stood over him, looking down at him.'

"Like my father said before me, he said, 'You trust everybody once."
Clement the Bloodhound

101

designing the creatures

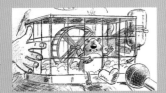

No matter how funny the interviews, how hilarious the voices and how off-beat the dialogue, the thousands of hours of interviews taken by the Aardman team and trained journalists up and down the country just take up shelf space and gather dust if they're not translated into something visual. Something ready for TV. The animators can't animate if they haven't got a Plasticine model to move, and the model-makers can't even start slapping Plasticine on the armatures if they haven't got a design to work from. The absolutely vital first step in translating the interviews into visual form is to sketch what the animals might look like. And that's where Michael Salter comes in.

Michael is one of Aardman's resident artists. He's been with the company for many years now, working on everything from Wallace and Gromit to *Chicken Run*, and over the course of time his style has grown more and more attuned to Aardman's needs.

Left: Name those Characters!
Below: Michael Salter works on the Norman character design (see page 100).
Opposite: More of Michael's character designs, pinned up on the walls of the model workshop as reference.
Below right: One of the monkeys being worked on.

'My style had similarities to Nick Park's,' he admits, 'but so many jobs came in that wanted the "Nick Park look" that I started doing it even more. And I can't do anything else now: it's sort of ingrained.'

Michael is brought in very early in the process, as he explains. 'They start with the interviews first, but as soon as they start thinking about how they're going to turn them into animation they want a visual, so they'll give me the brief. And sometimes I'll get to hear the voice of the interviewees but sometimes it's just, you know, "Go ahead and draw a monkey," without hearing them first.'

Hearing the voices does help Michael to visualize what he's doing, as he explains. 'We had some bloke from Norfolk and he was – what's the word when you think you have all the diseases under the sun? – a hypochondriac, and hearing his voice helped a lot. He had to be a blood-hound, very down at heel, with that lost dog look.'

Michael's work is surprisingly unconstrained by any requirements of the model-makers or animators, possibly because he is so experienced at designing for the animation process. 'When I first started,' he recalls, 'the model department always said, "Can you give us a front view, a top view and every sort of view you could think of," but that just

DANCING BEARS

"Oooh, hang on, hang on ... I won't let anyone stick a thermometer up my ... OW!"
Alvin the Dancing Bear

Above: Alvin the Dancing Bear, complete and ready for action.

took too long. Then the people who do the models got to the stage where they could instantly do a 3-D version without any help. A lot of their own ideas now go into it. And sometimes I look at what's come out and I think, I didn't quite figure it like *that*.'

Michael's probably worked on over one hundred designs for the new *Creature Comforts*, on everything from slugs, amoebae and worms to big cats, bears and extra-terrestrials. His favourite, however, is one of the less obvious ones. 'At the moment the one I like most is the hamster, the one who's in his cage with a bit of a chip on his shoulder. And he's always moaning about things. I like the sea lion as well: he's got a husky voice, and does a lot of horn blowing. They're my two favourites. And circus characters in general I quite like.'

Having worked on so many designs, there is a risk that Michael might start to run out of ideas. When Golly says, 'I want a monkey to go with this voice,' for instance, where does Michael start? How many different ways are there to draw a monkey?

'You've got all your different kinds of monkeys,' he adds, 'proboscis, chimp, baboon and the rest, so at least you can vary them. After a bit you end up looking through animal encyclopedias, and that's when you realize you really do need some help.'

'I look at what's come out and I think, I didn't quite figure it like that.'

Michael Salter

building the characters

For a woman who has spent years making things look as realistic as possible for adverts, TV productions and films, Kate Anderson initially found working as head of the large model construction team on *Creature Comforts* a bit worrying.

'The first thing Golly told us was, "Don't spend hours making things symmetrical, don't do it too well,"' she laughs. 'And after you've worked on *Chicken Run*, that can be quite a difficult thing. I now spend ages telling people, "Stop smoothing that off, stop making it look so perfect."'

As with any kind of creative team effort, there's an initial period when everyone has to work out what the joint style is, what they're all trying to achieve. With *Creature Comforts* they had the original Channel 4 version to look back to, but both Golly and Nick Park had strong ideas about what they now wanted.

'We had a chat with Nick at the beginning,' she remembers. 'We'd done a few characters, and we'd sculpted them with really wide mouths. And he said that the one thing that he didn't like is that they looked too forced because they had these big, grinning, Wallace mouths! So now we're being a bit more subtle.' Kate considers for a moment. 'I guess it

Above: Kate Anderson listens to Golly explain what he wants
Below: The model making workshop at Aardman.

'The first thing Golly told us was, "Don't spend hours making things symmetrical, don't do it too well."'
Kate Anderson

Above, left to right: Harriet Thomas and Tim the mole, Ben Greenwood and Bitzer the police dog, Chris Brock and a monkey's head, Claire Drewitt and a nervous alien. Left – Judging by the spot cream, the half-eaten pizza and the book on chat-up lines, Fluffy the hamster's owner is a teenage boy.

is the house style,' she says. 'There are certain things, like how you sculpt round the eyes, that I never really noticed until I did this job.'

Each creature takes between a week and three weeks to make, and they all start off looking pretty much the same. 'Well they've got very basic armatures,' Kate says, 'so they're literally just a lump of stuff with protruding wires for the arms and legs. If we think the models might break, we make them so that we can easily replace the wire, but things haven't been breaking very much probably because the models don't run around and jump or do anything very extreme. And then we decide what colour each creature's going to be. We give Golly a choice and he picks the one that he thinks looks nicest. Then we start building up the armature.'

And what they use to build the characters isn't some top-secret creation of a special effects lab., it's Plasticine. Simple Plasticine, the same stuff that's used in any kids nursery. Kate recalls, 'We started off at the beginning of *Creature Comforts* with the Plasticine that they sell in toy shops. After a while everyone was complaining that it was too sticky, so we started mixing in chalk to stiffen it up. But it ended up too crumbly. I think that's been the biggest nightmare – the Plasticine's either too soft, too hard, too crumbly, too sticky. Then it turned out that quite a few animators actually quite liked it soft. In fact they all have their own personal likes, including their favourite size of puppet and how stiff they like their armatures. So we've now started trying to custom-design the models when we've been told who is animating each character.'

'It astonishes me that the old bit of Plasticine we've been pushing around has suddenly almost become a living being.'
Kate Anderson

109

Right: Michael Salter's
2-D character design
for Miss Dynamite is
translated into 3-D
reality.
Below: They're red
(and green) and
wrapped in plastic!

The character-building team consists of seven people, including Kate, and she claims to be able to tell, just by looking at a model, who has built it. 'We've got Cath Ford, who's a trainee sculptor, and she's quite girlie – likes pink things – and what she's done so far is very feminine. She made a little mouse and you could see that it had been sculpted by a girl – no man would ever sculpt like that. And conversely some of the men do really nasty looking things with big teeth, creating vicious dogs, and things like that – so I try and give them things that I know they'll put their all into.'

Sometimes, of course, things don't quite work out as planned, as Kate recalls. 'Ben Greenwood recently made a security guard bulldog. In the original design it looked quite hard, but on listening to the voice it's apparent that it's actually more of a big softy so Ben changed it a little bit, to make him look less aggressive and more of an "all mouth and no trousers" kind of personality.'

The model-making team obviously works hard at creating characters and infusing them with personalities, liaising closely with the animators to provide them with something that'll survive under hot lights

As a bloodhound, Clement is used to being out in the cold and the damp for hours on end, chasing game and tracking quarry. That is probably why he suffers from so many ailments. That, or the amount of lead shot he has accidentally eaten over the years. He has heart palpitations, a swollen throat, problems with his eyes and various assorted allergies, as well as asthma and a dodgy inner-ear. There may well be more, but his memory is going as well.

Clement is a familiar figure in the local surgery, where he seems to spend most of his time waiting in queues. He feels — with some justification — that the staff have more or less given up on him, although every now and then they do send him for tests which he doesn't understand. The test that has him particularly confused is the eye test, where they clamp his head and bounce things off his eyeballs.

Clement particularly likes eating pheasant, but it has to be hung for four to five days to bring out the full flavour. This is an example of the extensive country lore that Clement used to possess but is progressively losing as his memory fails. Perhaps his biggest regret is that he has nobody to whom he can pass on his knowledge.

"What they do is they, they clamp your head in a, in a big clamp and they want to bounce things on your eyeballs, well, I can't, you know, I couldn't be doing with that."

Bottom: The two circus horses – Wilhelm II and Titania – are gradually constructed.

for weeks on end without cracking or falling apart, but the models aren't complete when they leave the model-makers' hands. There's one crucial last stage that they must go through before they can be animated – their mouths have to be made. All of them.

'We just make a kind of neutral mouth,' Kate says. 'It's supposed to be vaguely based on an "a" shape. That gets cut out, a mould is made, and then the assistant animators sculpt them into all the different mouth shapes for the animation. It never ceases to amaze me how they do that.'

Although Kate leads the model-building team, she also gets to build the models. Like a lot of people at Aardman, she enjoys the hands-on aspects of the work. 'Early on I did the sloth, the funny worm, and the sea lions, thousands of the damn things. I've quite got into making fat things, recently. I made an obese lady slug which I quite enjoyed, and fat seals!' She pauses a moment, reflecting on the many strange things about her job. 'It astonishes me,' she says, 'that the old bit of Plasticine we've been pushing around has suddenly almost become a living being.'

'I've quite got into making fat things recently. I made an obese lady slug which I quite enjoyed.'
Kate Anderson

lighting and filming

When the animator enters the little, screened-off studio area where he or she is going to work for the next few weeks, everything is carefully prepared. It's a quiet, rather solemn moment – the animator and the model. Of course, for a few days before that it was absolute chaos, with sets being nailed together and dressed, and then the lighting and camera crews coming in to set everything up.

Andy MacCormack is one of the two directors of photography on *Creature Comforts* (the other being Frank Passingham), which means it's his job to get on film exactly what the director wants. And that means everything from setting up the cameras to choosing the right lenses, to arranging the lighting to capture the right mood.

Andy has been with Aardman since the very early days, but the reason he joined the company had less to do with animation than a desire to keep working with film. 'To be perfectly honest,' he admits, 'that's the real reason. At that time broadcasters were turning to video and I was a very committed film man. And Pete Lord and David Sproxton were not only shooting on film, but 35mm-film which appealed to me even more.'

Ironically, the new *Creature Comforts* is being shot entirely digitally. No film is involved whatsoever. Surprisingly, Andy isn't too bothered – not now, at any rate, but it did initially cause some problems. 'First of all, I came to it with a load of luggage and attitude because, "It ain't got sprocket holes: it's the Devil's work!" What I was trying to do, I now realize, was to make digital technology look like film. Now that's a big one: everybody's trying to do that. And then after about one month I thought, this is daft. Instead of struggling to make it look like film, why don't I just accept the medium and make it look good for what it is? And as soon as I did that, it was an absolute breeze. But I still maintain, all those years ago, when I made that judgement call, that value judgement about whether to work on video or film, I was right.'

Andy's interest begins early in the production process when director Golly is deciding on the 'feel' of each film. 'Way back at the beginning,' Andy explains, 'when the sound edits are being done, Golly will decide, that this voice is a turtle, a donkey, whatever.'

Above: Andy Mack – an Aardman veteran. Below: Andy Mack's dog, Louise.

Following that decision, Golly will brief Michael Salter to draw a sketch of the character, sometimes based on an original design of Golly's. Golly approves the sketch, and now that piece of paper becomes vital. It goes to the model makers, and they build the model. Then it goes to the set builders, and they build the set in conjunction with me because whether we shoot it with a wide lens close-up, or a long lens far, far away, depends on the dimensions of the set. And when it comes to the lighting I'll say to Golly, "Give me a word on this one." And he'll say something like, "Oh, it's early evening with a fiery sky," or "It's a blood-red sunset," or "It's at night," and that'll give me a clue what it's gonna look like.'

With lights and cameras, as with almost every aspect of the work that Aardman does, animation brings its own unique set of problems. 'Nobody makes anything for animation,' Andy complains. 'It's too small a market. These cameras have not been made for animation: they've got a standard 10:1 zoom lens on them. So what we have to do is cheat the focal distance – the collimation on it – so that the cameras will now focus from 25cm (10in) to 4.5m (15ft), but they *won't* focus at infinity.'

Art director Kitty Clay and gaffer Clive Scott preparing the seagulls set.

'Way back at the beginning when the sound edits are being done, Golly will decide that this voice is a turtle, a donkey, whatever.'
Andy Mack

Similarly, Andy has to be creative with the lights. 'With live action,' he says, 'when a bulb breaks on set you just change the bulb. But with animation, if you've got a three-week shot and the bulb goes when you're two weeks in, you're potentially losing two weeks' worth of work.' That's because the bulbs heat up gradually and you don't notice the light change over the course of a shot. It gets warmer and warmer and then the bulb pops and it's replaced by a new one which is slightly darker. Having a bulb break half-way through shooting a scene can lead to a perceptible change in the quality of the light, and audiences are quick to pick up on things like that.

'And for that reason,' Andy adds, 'a lot of the lamps that we use are theatre, not film lamps, because theatre lighting is much more reliable. Bulbs last for weeks and weeks and weeks. The bulbs run at the equivalent of 250 or 260 volts, but when we run them at 230 volts they're effectively under-run and will last for a thousand hours. We also use smaller lamps: a lot of people call them 12 volters. We use an awful lot of those.'

Above: The time-consuming task of lighting the sets. Left and below: Richard 'Tricky' Hoskens at work. Even the lights have to be scaled down on some of the props.

dexter

"Wacky people ... just wacky people ... real strange."

'I actually go as far as sticking camera tape over the knobs, but they will take it off!'

Andy Mack

Above: Alvin's dressing room, lit and ready to go.
Below: The monitor immediately relays what the digital video camera sees – a huge advance over film technology.

Of course, besides all the technical challenges that Andy faces, there are the personal ones as well. The ones caused by the human need to fiddle. 'With film you have to test each shot,' he explains, 'because if you let the animators start without the test, and you shoot for two weeks on film and it's crap, it would be just awful. Of course, you don't have to do that on digital because what you see is what you get… pretty much. You do have to be a bit careful, though – the animators will fiddle around with the settings on their monitors so that they can see the picture better. And if I don't know that's happening and I'm creating lighting for a monitor that's been secretly turned up really bright, then the result is all black and murky. So I have to keep checking that they haven't cranked the brightness up. I actually go as far as sticking camera tape over the knobs, but they will take it off!'

the acting process

I t's hard for animators to work with no references, having nothing to fall back on in those long hours when they've forgotten whether the head of the model they are animating is meant to turn left or right. The director of a live-action drama has a script that specifies not only when a character enters a room and when it speaks, but also whether it's happy, sad or angry. The problem is that the model animators on *Creature Comforts* don't get a script, all they get is a transcript of the dialogue, and they then have to make their own decision about how it's said, which flickers of emotion need to be shown, and when to have blinks and twitches, and all those ingredients that make the models resemble real characters.

In order to help the animators, Golly uses a technique known as Live Action Video briefing (LAV). It provides the animators with a video

Digital editing – so much better than cutting bits of film and sticking them back together in a different order. The screen shows a recording from the LAV booth.

tape of themselves acting out the dialogue to a pre-recorded voice. The animators then use the tape as a reference – if the filmed face frowns and purses its lips when saying a particular line, the animators can make the model do the same.

The director, Golly, is keen on the LAV process. He believes it forms the cornerstone of the production process, allowing the animators to depict real movements and emotions. 'All the decisions about the acting and performance are made by reference to LAV. It helps you realize how people's expressions change. For example, when you speak your face gives away what you're about to say, and you might break into a smile before something funny. LAV helps us include these incredibly important little details and nuances.'

Golly is aware, though, that some of the animators working on *Creature Comforts* are uncomfortable with LAV. Unless you're an actor, you won't enjoy having your performance recorded for posterity (i.e. for the Aardman Christmas Party video). He is, however, completely convinced about its value.

'All the animators are different,' Golly continues. 'Some like to be filmed reading their lines, and some hate it and feel self-conscious, but it's a really worthwhile process. On video you can capture those little nuances of what happens to your eye line if you're lying, and where you look to visualize things and when you're trying to think of words. And the more human elements you put into the animation, the better it becomes.'

Above: In a rare moment of confusion, Golly attempts to tell the Plasticine models what to do. Below: The LAV process gives the animators a real sense of how Golly wants the creatures to move.

Some of the animators refuse point blank to appear in front of the camera, either through shyness or an awareness of their own acting limitations, and in these cases Golly has to step in and do the job himself. 'Yes, it's either them or me,' he admits. 'And it's quite often me because a lot of them don't like doing it. Then they'll direct me and talk to me about it, so I'll be sat on a chair reading their lines, and they'll be saying, "Oh no, I think you should do it like this."'

Jay Grace, one of the animators working on *Creature Comforts*, is one of the animators not particularly enamoured with LAV. 'I have to say it's not something that I particularly enjoy doing,' he says. 'Sometimes the lines are very long, so you might suddenly get given a thirty-second long piece of dialogue, and then you get wheeled into the video unit to rehearse it, but it's really hard remembering thirty-seconds' worth of dialogue while acting it.'

Jay is definitely one of the people who prefers it if Golly is the man with the camera being pointed at his face. 'I usually find it's easier to let Golly come up with an idea about how the script should be read,' Jay continues, 'because he knows the lines so well. And he has such a clear idea of what the characters are like that sometimes it's deviating from the path to do it yourself.'

Jay then uses that video of Golly reading out the lines so that it becomes the basis for his animation, but he's careful not to recreate slavishly what is on tape. There has to be some room for the animator's creative input. 'I think it's wrong to look at the video and try to replicate it exactly,' he says. 'And I'm also very aware that there are too many subtleties in the human face to try and capture them all, so you pick out the best ones and sift out the rubbish. If you put too much into the animation it starts to look a bit overdone and a bit dead. It's tempting, but you have to be restrained and pick the best ideas.'

There is, as Jay and the other animators are well aware, the possibility that the entire *Creature Comforts* could be recreated from the LAV tapes, with Golly, and those brave enough to step in front of the camera, pretending to be the bears, tigers, dogs and rats, as well as the aliens and plankton. 'It would be very entertaining,' Jay says, diplomatically. One cannot help but suspect, however, that he and the other animators intend getting hold of the master tapes and burning them, rather than let them creep out as special features on the *Creature Comforts* DVD release.

> *'I have to say it's not something that I particularly enjoy doing.'*
> **Jay Grace**

Spanner and Trousers being animated – the monitor in the background shows the camera's view.

the animation process

The pre-production phase for any episode of *Creature Comforts* is filled with people interviewing, transcribing, sound editing, designing, model making and holding meetings. The post-production phase is similarly filled with people editing the visuals, cranking up the huge publicity machine and holding more meetings. In the middle, however, comes the production phase which involves working alone in a small wooden cubicle for weeks, if not months, on end.

Jay Grace is one of the many talented model animators at Aardman, and he is directly responsible for the things that will appear on screen. If there are fingerprints visible on the models, they are his fingerprints. Jay wasn't at Aardman when the original *Creature Comforts* was made, but seeing it led to his career as an animator and to him working on its successor.

'I was in my first year at college and I remember seeing it on my little black and white TV in my halls of residence room and thinking it was amazing. It was so fresh. That was one of the things that inspired me to go into animation.'

Chappy, the retired cart-horse, leaning on the fence at Sunny Villa Farm.

Jay's involvement with the production phase starts pretty late in the day. 'Normally the models have been designed and given a character. I usually get involved when it's just about time to start filming and I'll get a list of the things I've got to do. I start with the LAV where Golly and I act through the lines.' When the LAV tape is ready, Jay enters the small cubicle where the animation will take place.

'The camera team usually put the set in and they'll frame the shot, and put the puppet in an approximate position that's good for them, compositionally.' There are, however, certain preparations Jay has to make before he can actually start work.

'When the model comes straight out of model making it's usually pristine and in a fixed pose,' he reveals, 'so you try to personalize it a bit, and maybe adjust the face so it's the way you like. That's pretty much what I spend the first day doing, and adjusting the mouths to make sure that they all fit properly.'

These mouths are a set of alternative mouths covering different phonetic sounds. They slot into a gap left by the model makers between the character's chin and nose (or beak, proboscis, or whatever), and the animators sculpt them in so that the join is invisible.

'You try to personalize it a bit, and maybe adjust the face so it's the way you like.'

Jay Grace

Above: Chappy, seen from the back, showing that the models are only as complete as they need to be for the chosen camera angle. Overleaf: A long shot of Chappy's paddock, revealing how the perspective on the shot is achieved.

123

'I tend to work with about ten or twelve mouths,' says Jay. 'Some people like to make a mouth for every possible eventuality, and might have 20 mouths on their set. But we also do a lot of what we call "sculpting through", where you leave the same mouth on because it's easier to push the same one around. That's how Nick Park used to work. He didn't have replacements when he did the original *Creature Comforts*: he would just have the same puppet on set and change its mouth from an "ee" to an "oo."'

It's crucial that all the mouths look the same so that when the animator switches from one to another it doesn't appear obvious on screen. This usually takes a bit of sorting out. 'I normally work with an assistant who will buff up the mouths,' Jay reveals, 'and then usually, on that first day, when you get on set with the character, you spend a bit of time getting the mouths to fit and look right. Hopefully, by the end of the first day, you've been through all the mouths and they're working okay. It really does speed things up.'

Once the preparations are complete, the model has been roughed up a bit and the mouths have been fitted and made to look as if they belong to the same animal, then the animation can start. And, given the nature of *Creature Comforts*, that mostly means animating for dialogue and not complicated gestures.

'The characters are locked in place and are built very solidly so you can't do an awful lot,' Jay admits, 'you can just move their heads around. You really have to think about what you're doing with the eyes and the face though, because that's where the character comes from.'

The actual process followed by the animators is oddly mundane. 'You then listen to the sound-track, over and over, and look at the video tape, and try to plan the highs and lows of the shot so that it's not monotonously paced. And then you get stuck in. You just shoot until it's finished!'

Matching the movements of the Plasticine lips with the syllables, the odd little 'hmms' and 'aaahs', the laughs and the sighs, seems from the outside to be a mysterious art. But from Jay's point of view, it's simple. 'Before I learned how to do it, it seemed incredibly difficult,' he agrees. 'But when you actually look at it, you have your soundtrack broken down phonetically, and you listen to the track very carefully, and then you just have to move the mouth to fit that sound. It sounds simplistic, but that's it.'

"No, don't want to burn my skin, do I? Bad for you!"

Anthony the Pig

Anthony the Pig has his mouth adjusted to form a particular syllable.

Chappy's life as a horse has been long and hard and, as he heads toward a well-earned retirement, he takes some pleasure in looking back on the many tasks he has performed, and in passing his advice onto anyone who will stop and listen.

Cursed with bad health, Chappy has seen his fair share of medics and hasn't been impressed. He's been prescribed a lot of medication over the years, but he does consider himself lucky that he's still alive. He has been advised not to go out on cold mornings or in the wind, and finds it difficult to walk uphill without getting chest pains. If he has to go down to the Co-op for any reason, then he usually gets the bus back home again.

Home for Chappy is Sunny Villa Farm, where he lives a life of quiet reflection, with the occasional trip out to pull a cart for the local children. On these trips he usually wears a straw hat with a flower in the brim. He considers this to be undignified.

Chappy's main concern is the quality of the food that children eat these days. He feels that the food has too much fat in it, and thinks that instead of kiddies buying chips for their lunch they should buy a couple of apples, or a couple of pears.

As far as Chappy is concerned, his ideal day would be dry, with a temperature of 18.5–20°C (65–68°F).

"I've took a lot of tablets all my life, err, about 23,000 and I'm still alive, but uh, at the end of the day I think without them I'd have been dead."

"The trouble with the food we eat now, there's too much fat in 'em, and the worst thing that happens in this country, there's too many people eat chips."

Chappy

The soundtracks that Jay and the other animators use are digital, and they can be used in their cubicles in a range of ways, for example skipping back and forth, enabling them to concentrate on specific fragments of sound. 'In comparison to how Nick and the guys used to work fifteen years ago, it's much, much simpler,' says Jay, thankfully. 'In the old days they used to have an old cassette recorder and had to press the button when the model started to talk on the screen. Now everything is much slicker.'

Time stretches when you're doing animation. Small, almost unnoticeable gestures such as a blink or a twitch, occupying fractions of a second from an audience's point of view, can preoccupy an animator for hours to the exclusion of everything else. 'We work on the basis of doing between three and five seconds a day,' Jay says, 'and, on average, the individual shots seem to last from fifteen to twenty seconds. So it takes four days to finish one fifteen-second shot. It's quite a quick

Darren Thompson working with the seagulls.

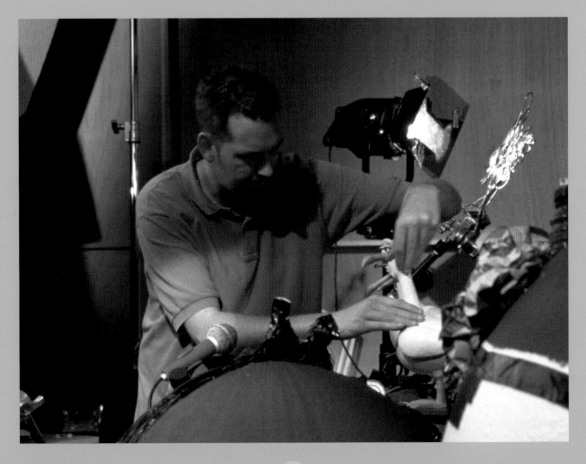

A program called Animate is used to create broadcast-quality single frames of animation .

turnaround compared to how we shoot features such as *Chicken Run* where we normally produce four seconds a week.'

The problem with working at this speed – if speed is the right word – is that there isn't normally time to go back and change what you've done if you don't like it. 'You've pretty much got to live with it,' Jay agrees. 'But when you look at it a few weeks later, you wonder what you were worried about. I stand 30cm (1ft) away from my monitor where I can see the minute details, and there will be things that really irritate me, but to the untrained eye they aren't noticeable. But when you watch it with a crowd of people and they laugh when they're supposed to, that's worth ten bad days.'

Of course, advances in technology mean that mistakes can be erased or bypassed, not something that Nick Park could do on the original *Creature Comforts*. The new series is entirely digital, and that makes Jay's life significantly easier. 'When shooting on video you have the opportunity to rub out frames which you don't have when using film. And on film, once you press the button, that's it. You have to put a huge board in saying, "I've made a mistake" if you want to get rid of any frames.'

Although *Creature Comforts* is meant to have a consistent style for all the animals, Jay agrees with Nick and Golly that each animator has his or her own distinctive approach. 'Looking at *Creature Comforts*, I can pretty much pick out who has done what because we all have certain mannerisms that we use, like a store of gestures and eye movements. It's funny, because you can spot the person in the character. And then the characters start to look like the person – it's really strange.'

Of course, the longer an animator spends working on a particular character, the more obsessed he becomes. In order to avoid the

'The characters are locked in place... so you can't do an awful lot... You have to think about what you're doing with the eyes and the face though, because that's where the character comes from.'

Jay Grace

129

  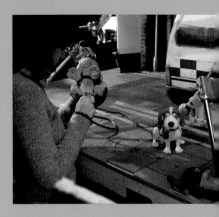

problem, and to keep the animators fresh, Golly makes sure that now and again they swap models. Jay explains, 'It helps if you're switching from character to character, and you get a fresh perspective. If you're just animating the same character, day in, day out, over and over again, it does get repetitive, and it's hard to come up with fresh ideas. There are animators in the studio that have worked on the same character for fifteen weeks. That's pretty demanding stuff.'

Jay's favourite character is, surprisingly, one of the simplest ones, and yet the one that provided him with his greatest challenge. 'I started off animating a very depressed worm,' Jay says, 'who seemed to live with his mother. Actually, I really like the worm. It's funny because, when I saw it, it was just a 30cm (12in) high, pink-ribbed worm. It didn't have eyes, it didn't have the "Nick Park" brows, it just had a really depressing voice, and I thought that's gonna be really hard. But he had some really funny lines in the end, and I enjoyed it.'

Recalling some of the other characters he has animated, Jay begins to suspect that he has been typecast. 'I did a couple of miserable donkeys on a beach, and a miserable old horse as well. And I'm animating a shark at the moment who's completely insane.'

He laughs, but there's a hint of worry in the laugh. 'There's definitely a theme there,' he says.

Some of the animators at work. Above, left to right: Ian Whitlock and Martin the fly; Chris Sadler and Fluffy; Claire Billet; Andy Symanowski; Terry Brain; Seamus Malone. Below, left to right: Dan Ramsay and Sapphire the dolphin; Suzy Fagan with Sue and Lorraine, the walruses; Lee Wilton. Opposite: an unfinished donkey model – either Banjo or Sparkle.

 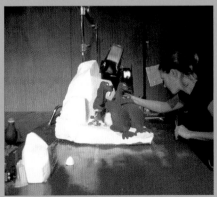 

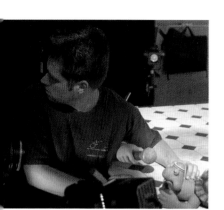

problems with animation

Gary and Nigel struggle in the 'snow'.

Plasticine has certain advantages over real people – it doesn't have tantrums, doesn't give a bad performance and it doesn't fluff a line. Every performance is as perfect as the animator can manage. Just imagine ITV's *It'll Be Alright on the Night* with stop-motion animated figures – it's difficult, isn't it?

On the other hand, Plasticine, as anyone on the Aardman team will tell you, is a temperamental beast. Andy Mack, director of photography on *Creature Comforts*, is not its greatest fan and he's been with Aardman for the best part of twenty-five years. 'If you paid a consultant materials designer a vast sum of money to come up with the worst possible material for animating,' Andy sighs, 'he'd definitely come up with Plasticine.'

'A company used to make a special mix for Aardman,' reveals production manager Gareth Owen, 'but when they stopped doing that mix, it caused a big problem. We need our "Wallace-style" Plasticine, so now we have a woman who specially comes in to mix our own blend of Plasticine.'

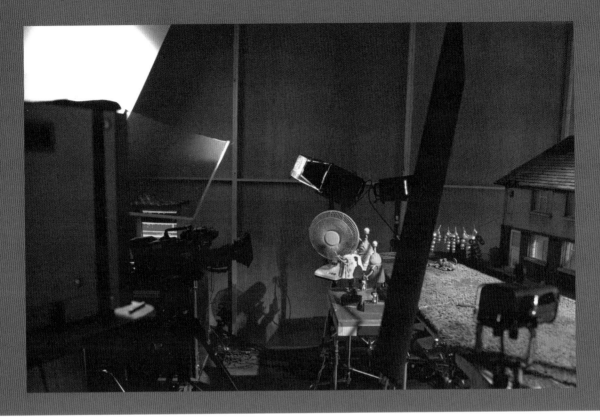

To the uninitiated, Plasticine is Plasticine, but to the expert eye there are a thousand different varieties and types. 'The texture of the Plasticine does vary,' Gareth continues. 'Black Plasticine, for instance, tends to be softer, but as you go towards the lighter shades it tends to get a bit harder. We've had to experiment with our own mix but we didn't get it right with the first few puppets, some were really soft and too difficult to animate. And then, of course, you've got the different animators' requests, with some of them liking it on the soft side, some hard.'

Kate Anderson, head of the model-making team, has her own concerns about Plasticine. 'If you start putting too many different colours on any character,' she says, 'the shades of Plasticine can get blended together because the animator keeps touching it, and it gives a kind of "boiling" effect which can look nice, but it doesn't look particularly professional. We did these scavenger dogs, for instance – there's a white one and a brown one – but every time the animator touched one puppet he'd have to clean his hands before he could touch the next puppet, otherwise he'd get brown all over the white one, and *vice versa*.'

'No, you can't have Plasticine that's several different colours,' confirms director Golly, 'because as you're animating they're all going to merge.' Kate agrees, 'Simplicity is one of our watch-words. You don't want things to get too fussy with the colours or as regards anything else. That'd then mean that the animators couldn't do certain things, or that they'd run out of time.

> '*Simplicity is one of our watch-words. You don't want things to get too fussy with the colours.*'
>
> **Kate Anderson**

The same shot, but seen from the front. Compare this with the shot on page 88.

Sometimes, though, Golly will say, "No, I want pink hands and brown bodies," and if that's what he wants, we do it. You don't compromise the design.'

Temperature is probably the biggest enemy of the Aardman team. Plasticine doesn't react well to heat because it becomes sticky and loses its rigidity. So, having hot lights pointing at the models for hours on end isn't ideal because the arms droop, expressions wilt, and something that looked fresh at the start of the day ends up looking pretty tired. The studio environment is air-conditioned in an attempt to minimize this effect but, even so, the small units in which the animators work can get rather uncomfortable.

The problem has existed since Aardman's beginnings, as Andy Mack reveals. 'I've known Peter Lord have two Morphs which he'll fix in the same position. One will live in the fridge, and when the other one gets a bit steamy he'll fetch it out.'

But the Plasticine isn't the only thing that reacts to the heat. Golly continues, 'It doesn't matter what materials you use for the sets, whether its wood or steel, because both react to temperature change, no matter what you do. Sometimes sets will stay completely stable, and sometimes they'll move quite dramatically in lots of different directions!'

" The first few months in this country I had to learn that you do not kiss everybody to say hello. And I did with the postman . "
Mother Alien

Originally urban loft dwellers, Sid and Nancy recently relocated to a west-facing Hackney potting shed. Since the move the couple have noticed a marked improvement in their sleep patterns, and feel that the sheltered location provides a perfect setting within which to raise a family.

Sid has always wanted a garden shed, and now is quite happy to while away the days listening to the radio. Nancy often jokes that he has a stash of pornography hidden away somewhere inside, but she can't prove it. Maybe she is joking, or maybe she isn't.

Sid is a hypochondriac, often imagining that nagging pains or twinges are often something really serious, but he never actually goes to the doctor about it. Nancy jokes that he never shuts up about it either, but – as usual with Nancy – it's difficult to tell whether she's really joking or not.

"I've always wanted a shed all my life and now I've got one."

sid & nancy

Anthony the Pig, posed in front of a blue sky backdrop. The sheer amount of equipment surrounding the model shows the scale of the production process.

That could be catastrophic because the cameras and sets have to be locked in position so that the background is in exactly the same position right through the shoot. And besides the temperature changes caused by the heat of the lights, bulbs can cause huge problems (see page 116).

Despite Golly's oft-repeated insistence that the models should have a quirky, hand-built look, the production values on *Creature Comforts* are impressively high. Yes, he'll tolerate some finger marks but not flickering lights or sliding sets.

Nick Park is very clear, though, about the advantages of possible problems. 'Sometimes having limitations forces you to be more creative. That's why I really enjoyed doing the original *Creature Comforts* film and that's why I like what they're doing now with the new series.'

'Sometimes having limitations forces you to be more creative.'
Nick Park

computer-generated characters

Below: Stephan
Marjoram.
Opposite: The
plankton.

Mention Aardman to people in the street – or just the name Nick Park – and more often than not they say, 'Oh yes, the Plasticine figures.' Because of the association that's been built up over the years, from Morph through *Creature Comforts* and Wallace and Gromit to *Chicken Run*, people assume that's all that Aardman does. But no longer. There is, dare we say it, a hint of heresy in the air. Computer-generated characters have reportedly been seen on the premises. And they're the responsibility of a man named Stefan Marjoram.

There's already a degree of computer post-production in *Creature Comforts*. With luck, most of it will be unnoticeable, as it consists of removing wires and supports ('rigging') and placing characters in environments such as water. Stefan's job, however, is more obvious – he makes actual characters in his computer.

Stefan joined Aardman after previous spells at a computer-games company and with the BBC. Having previously created some computer-animated characters for a potential direct-to-video spin-off from *Chicken Run*, and then worked on computer-generated blobs that have been used on the new digital BBC3 channel, Stefan was asked to join *Creature Comforts*. They wanted a character that couldn't be built in the Aardman workshop – a microscopic member of the plankton family.

'A character like this, with tentacles all the way around it, and small fur-like nodules, would be a nightmare in Plasticine,' Stefan explains, 'because you've got ten tentacles to animate, and there'd always be a danger of nudging the fur.'

The origins of the character were very similar to those of the other creatures in *Creature Comforts*. 'I drew a page of various kinds of plankton,' Stefan explains, 'just a page of doodles really. Golly picked a few that he quite liked, and then he drew the mouths that he wanted. That meant they'd fit in with the other characters that had been made.

'The creature is meant to be in the foreground talking,' says Stefan, 'while these other things are floating around and bobbing up in the background, and sometimes going through each other and eating each other. I suppose the main reason for their being computer-generated rather

> *'A character like this, with tentacles all the way around it and small fur-like nodules, would be a nightmare in Plasticine.'*
> **Stefan Marjoram**

than Plasticine is because they all have to have that distinctive, translucent feel.'

Computer animation is, as Stefan explains, a lot more forgiving than the 3-dimensional animation that's being used in the rest of *Creature Comforts*. 'You can plan a movement and glide your character through the scene without bothering about the legs or anything else, just to see whether he moves at the right speed. And then you can overlay the leg animation so that his feet are doing the right thing. Then you go back and do the upper and lower arms, and the fingers. Same with the face – you do the head, then the mouth, and then the detail with the eyes and eyelids. You keep adding different layers whereas with model animation you get one try, and you do everything at once.'

The process does, however, depend on there being enough time to add all the layers. 'If you're a bit tight for time you could get the body working right and then concentrate on a few things like the eyes – everybody looks at the eyes to try and read the emotions. But *Creature*

"I regard myself as a kind of ego-driven space-time meat vehicle."
Brian

Comforts has got a reputation that I have got to live up to, and this, their first computer-generated character, has got to be something that they're very happy with. So I am adding every detail!'

The one element that can never be skipped is the matching of mouth movements to the pre-recorded voices, but even here Stefan has some tricks that make the process smoother. 'The stop-motion animator will have a drawer full of Plasticine mouths that he can use, whereas I make a mouth and duplicate it, creating all these different shapes.'

Working with the computer, Stefan is working slightly faster (producing about ten seconds of film a day) than the model animators (producing around three to five seconds). 'One reason I'm faster is that I've found a clever way of doing the tentacles automatically, and I've got a friend of mine, Dave, animating the background characters.'

One of the key design elements that director Golly has been attempting to bring into *Creature Comforts* is the idea that things don't have to be perfect, that finger marks and smudges are okay. This, of

> "I love smiling, I love being happy, being jovial, telling jokes, being the butt end of jokes but hey, now I can do it with a mouth full of teeth and I'm really looking forward to it."
>
> **Precious the piranha**

> '**Whenever anybody builds anything for me, I always have to sort of wonkify it a bit.**'
>
> **Stefan Marjoram**

The upper reaches of the circus tent, before and after Matilda is added.

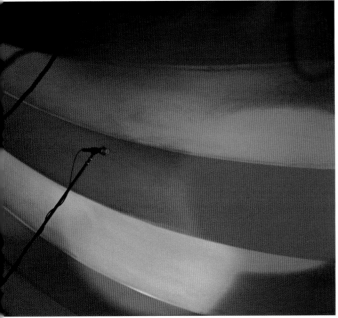

course, goes completely against the usual tenets of computer animation, where everything is clean and smooth. With normal model
animation you have to work hard to make it look perfect. With computer
animation you have to work hard so that it does *not* look perfect.

According to Stefan, 'When you build something, it's so easy to
build everything symmetrically. There's even a symmetry button so that
whatever you do on one side happens on the other. But whenever
anybody builds anything for me, I always have to sort of wonkify it a bit,
making one finger slightly longer than another, for example!'

Although Stefan trained as a 2-dimensional animator, working
alongside an ex-Disney expert, he strongly feels that he's found his place
with computer animation. 'With a computer you can have every job that's
involved in making a film at your fingertips. You can light, position the
cameras, paint the sets and texture them, even do the sculpting,' he
laughs. 'With computers you can be a megalomaniac.'

Precious the Piranha, posed against a blue screen. A watery background will be added later, in post-production, and the rigging removed using computer technology.

the editing process

In normal television, if there is such a thing, the editing process is almost the last thing that happens. All the filming or video-taping has been done, the performances are fixed on several miles of video tape, and all that remains is for the editor to be locked in a room and painstakingly assemble the final product.

But *Creature Comforts* is different. For a start, the editing is done at the same time as the filming, or even before it, in some cases, because the episodes are constructed in audio form even before any decisions have been made as to which animals will be talking.

Dan Lincoln is one of those people responsible for editing all the material collected for the thirteen episodes of *Creature Comforts* into a coherent form. 'The first thing I do,' he explains, 'is listen to a CD of the audio material from an interview and look at the corresponding transcript. The transcript is marked up by Golly or Toby Farrow, and I take line selections and put them into a rough edit.'

The ratio of material that goes in to the editing process compared with the material that comes out is high. 'I get up to an hour and a half, perhaps two hours, of audio clips which it's thought might work and then I've got to get it down to eight minutes. It's quite easy to start picking off the stuff that's definitely not working, and then you get it down to about twenty minutes. But twenty minutes down to eight minutes is the most difficult bit.'

And it's not just a question of using all the funniest bits and stringing them together. That would be like having a stand-up act composed entirely of punch lines. In order to make the funny bits stand out, they often need more serious, reflective lines around them. 'Sometimes you choose all the highlights and put them in a pile and try and fit them together,' Dan says, 'then realize that they need tempering with more sober pieces.'

Dan Lincoln and Toby Farrow work on more interview material.

'I get two hours of clips which it's thought might work, and then I've got to get it down to eight minutes.'
Dan Lincoln

Once an episode has been roughly assembled, one of the editors then sits down with Golly and reviews the dialogue with the original sketches, creating a simple film called an animatic. It is at this point that the suitability of the chosen visual designs for the dialogue is assessed.

'Suddenly a voice that was supposed to be a chicken now sounds more like a Vietnamese pot-bellied pig,' Dan explains. '*Why* it should sound like that, you don't know. But you think, "Okay! Let's try that." And then, as soon as you put a picture to it you can tell whether it's going to work as a character.'

Dan had originally hoped that, once they had finished assembling the first episode, they would have a template to follow for the rest. It hasn't worked out like that because every episode is structured in a different way.

'I was chatting to Terry, one of the animators,' Dan says, 'and the *Aliens* episode seems to him to be almost *X-Files*: slightly dramatic, almost taking you somewhere unusual. And *Pets at the Vets* is pure stand-up comedy, almost slapstick, because it's people talking about their ailments. But things that you thought were going to be really funny sometimes come over as quite tragic, and things that you thought were so risqué that they shouldn't go in, everyone seems to lap up. What's so exciting about the whole series is the variety, with characters changing from one episode to another. And because at the editing stage you're looking at the pieces and then trying to see what picture they might make. Nothing's decided in advance.'

Once the audio edit is complete, and the animators start producing their four seconds a day of animated creatures, Dan can put the two together, matching the moving lips to the sounds.

Eight minutes of film doesn't sound a lot, but when you remember that Dan had an hour-and-a-half to two hours of material per character to whittle down, then you can realize how much work is involved.

'As Golly keeps reminding us,' Dan says, proudly, 'it's a whole feature film's worth of animation!'

"An unidentifying object ... no, I've never seen one of those I don't even know what one is."
Pickles the Guide Dog

'Suddenly a voice that was supposed to be a chicken now sounds more like a Vietnamese pot-bellied pig.'
Dan Lincoln

art direction

A large part of the charm of the original *Creature Comforts*, and one of the main reasons for its success, was the look of the world that Nick Park and Aardman created. Everything was simplified and perfectly scaled down to the size of the animals. Nothing was cluttered or confusing, and everything was designed to direct attention straight to the Plasticine stars.

The new *Creature Comforts* attempts to match the design of the original while making it look contemporary rather than old fashioned. And in this version of *Creature Comforts* there are significantly more sets and props to build. The key to this process is Kitty Clay, the aptly named art director.

'It's up to me to make sure that everything comes together and creates the right look for *Creature Comforts*-land,' she explains. 'I've got to make sure that all the props get made, and that the characters are just the right size.'

Unlike the sanitized, perfect world of most contemporary animation, the creative team at Aardman have been given strict guidance by director Golly which makes it clear that he wants it to look like it's been "thumbed". In other words, it should look like it has actually been made by hand and not high-tech tools.

Golly and Andy Mack discuss lighting and camera issues with Kitty Clay.

Relative size is another key issue when constructing for the new series. One of the problems faced by Kitty and her team is that background wallpaper, or a tea cup, or a table constructed for one character might not suit another. 'Each of the sets are different sizes,' she says. 'On one set you might have slugs which are 7.5cm (3in) tall, and on another a dog which is 10cm (4in) tall. The skill is in making sure that they all look like they belong in the same world.'

The sets that the animals inhabit are meant to look like ordinary, everyday places – homes, gardens, alleyways and shops – but they all have to be constructed from scratch, either being built from new or from small items that were originally intended for something else entirely.

'We have boxes of bits and bobs left over from other jobs,' says Kitty, 'and you'll rummage through those. Or you can spend hours going around lots of different shops trying to find a particular item. One of the animators said it's just like working on a school play because you find something and think, yes, that'll do.'

One of the options, of course, is to use something that was constructed for another purpose entirely. 'There's a doll's house shop in Bristol,' Kitty explains, 'and on one of the sets I've managed to use wallpaper from one of its toy houses, but in most cases it's probably better to make it yourself because then you get exactly the right design and colours.'

Creating scaled-down wallpaper from scratch usually means designing it on a computer. 'You can then print it onto watercolour paper, and add some colour to make it look old and slightly faded,' Kitty reveals. There is an alternative, but not one that Kitty favours. 'I haven't done this, but you can hand paint sheets of wallpaper, which would take absolutely ages!'

'One of the animators said it's just like working on a school play...'
Kitty Clay

Kitty Clay and Justine Bailey build a beach for Megan and Gladys the seagulls.

Nobody can distinguish Muzulu and Toto, the performing monkeys, apart any more. They look the same, talk the same and finish each other's sentences to the extent that it's hard to tell where one stops and the other starts. They are codependent, reliant on each other's company despite their frequent spats.

Neither Muzulu nor Toto are sure any more whether the actual performing still excites them or whether its just about the money. Whatever the lure, the two of them rehearse constantly when they are on the road, touring, staying up all night long practising their handstands, spending hours balancing and tumbling and helping each other learn tricks.

Muzulu has, during the course of his performing career, broken all his toes, damaged his knee, bust both of his ankles, broken his hand and wrist, smashed his collar bones several times, bashed his head and knackered his back, but he still feels it's all been worth it. Toto's list of injuries is similar, but he doesn't feel the need to boast about them.

"I've had crabs, they were good.'"
"They got out of hand didn't they?"
"They did, yeah."

"If you had six legs, where would your Arsenal be?"

mazulu & toto

Possibly the greatest of the many unusual challenges Kitty has faced working on *Creature Comforts* is making a set to house the dog fleas. 'That's quite a strange one,' she recalls. 'It's a huge set – about 1.2m (4ft) deep – showing all the pores where the hair comes out of the dog, and we've got flea eggs, and fleas which are about 15–18cm (6–7in) tall. The hairs at the front are probably about 7.5–10cm (3–4in) wide, and the ones at the back are about 2.5cm (1in) wide. That set actually took a hell of a long time to make because we had to sculpt the skin surface, then dress it up, and paint it. Each of the hairs had to be hand painted and sprayed, and then we put on a protective gloss coating to stop the paint from falling off. With three or four of us working on it, it took two to three weeks.'

But of all of the work Kitty has done on *Creature Comforts*, it's one of the simpler jobs that sticks out in her mind. 'We had three huge bears in ballerina outfits. The set was a marquee and a dressing table with lights round the edge of it, and it was very nicely lit.'

Kitty is clear about the appeal of the series. 'If you see the original black and white drawings,' she says, 'you're laughing already; you're thinking they're really funny! And then you see the puppets being made and you think they're really good, and then you get to the stage when they're animated, and you can hear what they're saying, it's just so funny. I've seen it all loads of times now, and I'm still laughing.'

'I've seen it all loads of times now, and I'm still laughing.'

Kitty Clay

"Horse poo is very good, you know, but human poo and dog poo that's poisonous I think"

Martin the Fly

Below: Chappy gets some time away from his paddock. Everything here – the road, the railings, the cart, the houses and the greenery – has to be created from scratch.

"Dogs I like very much because of their great intelligence and loyalty..."

One of the odd things about film and television is the discrepancy in terms of energy: so much effort and time is directed at one or two people standing in a half-built room, for example, while swapping a few lines of dialogue. In *Creature Comforts* the discrepancy is even more marked: there's a similar burst of energy on one side of the camera from the people responsible for constructing, rigging and preparing everything, but on the other side there's just some coloured clay.

Gareth Owen is the production manager for *Creature Comforts*. With a background working on other Aardman animated productions, Gareth finds that the

Above: Gareth Owen, planning out the production process. Right: Planning which elements of *Creature Comforts* are being animated where, and when.

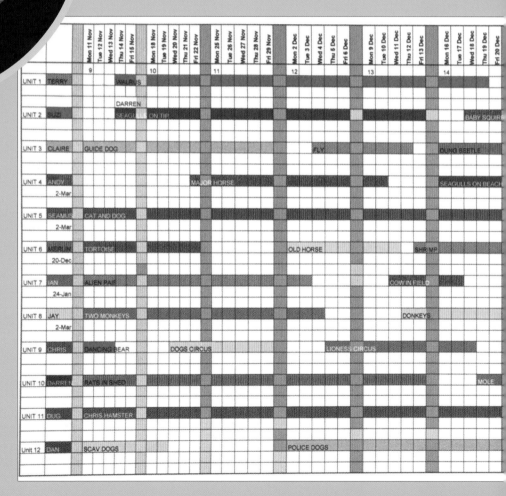

organizational aspects of coordinating all the practical elements of the shoot suit him perfectly.

'I manage all aspects of the production,' he says, 'from organizing the art department, getting the sets and the models made, hiring the floor crew, organizing the equipment and lighting, and making sure that everything we need for the shoot is there, on time and on budget.'

Unlike many of the other people working on *Creature Comforts*, who tend to work individually, Gareth has to worry about an entire team. 'There's a vague kind of hierarchy,' he reveals. 'You've got your director of photography (DOP) who is responsible for lighting the sets. We've got a couple of camera assistants. And then there's a lighting electrician who works directly under the DOP and he'll say, "I want this light or that filter." There's the floor manager who is responsible for checking that the sets are on bases, and getting daily reports from the animators. And then there are the four set dressers

> "Just so long as its filling and barely edible, I'll pretty much eat it, I'm always too hungry to be picky."
> **Dennis the Dung Beetle**

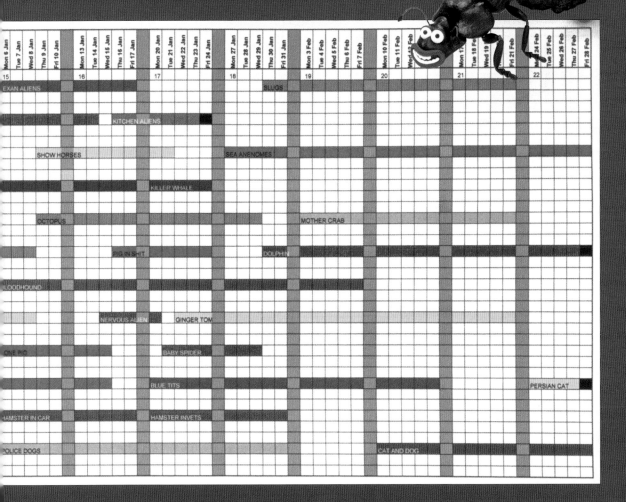

Pickles the guide dog gets a lot of pleasure from helping people achieve more mobility. Her Good Samaritan principles derive from her strongly held religious principles. She holds no truck with evolution or with the idea of intelligent life elsewhere in the universe, believing that mankind – and indeed dogs – are descended from Adam and Eve, and that God would not create anything that was not perfect.

Pickles has some strange opinions about food. She believes that spam, for instance, is a mixture of sheep's eyeballs, cow intestines and other, less savoury, bits of animals, all mixed together.

Usually calm and reliable, Pickles has been known to lapse into romantic slushiness at Christmas. She once tried to accost the caretaker of her flats with mistletoe in the car park, but he was a fast runner and managed to get away from her before she could kiss him.

"You may as well enjoy life because you don't live for very long."

pickles

who prepare the sets.' Gareth also has to work as fast as he can to keep up with a situation that can change from day to day, hour to hour or moment to moment.

'I suppose the most difficult part of my job is scheduling some shots while editing the episodes that they're meant to go in. And right now it's getting harder as we go on. But hopefully in the next month we'll have caught up on the editing.' Gareth shakes his head in resignation. 'And then, I'll spend at least half my time re-scheduling the model makers, the sets being built, models being built, and the dates for the breakdown of the voice track for the animators to animate."

The key to the scheduling process is an accurate estimation of how much usable material the animators can produce per day. 'You get to know what people's rates are, and you then have to make educated guesses as to how fast they're going to be working on certain puppets. Some puppets talk really quickly, but if they've got a pair that are talking at the same time, it's going to slow them down quite substantially.'

The scale of the production is much, much bigger than the original *Creature Comforts*. According to Gareth, 'Our sets and characters are a lot more complicated and more intricate. Fortunately, everyone is having a good time which helps diffuse any tension that might arise. In fact, it's been a pretty relaxed atmosphere. And one way of keeping the crew motivated is to show them every week what's been shot, and everyone sees what we're working towards.'

Gareth smiles as he sums up the appeal of *Creature Comforts* not only for the people, like him, who are working on it, but also for the people who will be watching and rewatching it for years to come. 'That's the joy of what we're doing,' he says. 'Seeing real things happening to real people put into the mouths of silly Plasticine puppets!'

"Freddie Starr couldn't pay enough for us, that was the highlight of our career I think."
Mazulu

'That's the joy of what we're doing. Seeing real things happening to real people put into the mouths of silly Plasticine puppets!'
Gareth Owen

sound effects

A lot of what's done at the Aardman studios is what one might consider 'obvious stuff' – things you can see on screen, like the models and the sets, and the things you can hear the characters saying. Somewhere underneath that, however, there's another layer, a layer of stuff you might not notice the first, or second, or fifth time you watch an episode, but which supports the obvious stuff and would be missed if it wasn't there.

A prime example of 'non-obvious stuff' is the sound effects that are present in every episode. These might range from the subtle background bubbling of water when the piranha is on screen to the squawk of gulls when Megan and Gladys are talking. They're all added on fairly late in the day, and James Mather is the man primarily responsible.

James's responsibilities go much wider than just the sound effects, however. As Supervising Sound Editor, he is the man who, more than anyone else, has created the aural style for the series. From the initial choice of voices through to the sound of an alien spacecraft taking off, James has been an integral part of *Creature Comforts* from the word go – and even before that.

'My role on *Creature Comforts* was established at an early stage of the process,' James explains. 'Golly and I put together a short pilot to sell the idea, and to address the logistics of a series of this scale. While editing the dialogues for the story artists to create creature designs, Golly and I considered which voices suited which animals and what style we might adopt.'

James first became involved with Aardman in 1983 when he worked as an assistant film editor on the *Animated Conversations* series. He began sound editing for them in 1991 on various commercials and then short films such as *Humdrum*, *Stage Fright* and *Wats' Pig*. This led on to series work with *Rex the Runt* and now *Creature Comforts*. Somewhere in amongst these projects he also managed to squeeze in the sound supervision on *Chicken Run*.

Once *Creature Comforts* was commissioned, James and Golly – along with Joseph Stracey, the Assistant Sound Editor – set forth listening to tapes, reading transcriptions and editing the mass of recordings which started to appear.

'Before each batch,' James says, 'a small group of us would sit around a table and thrash out potential subjects for the team of recordists to address. We also attempted to write questions which we hoped would give us entertaining answers. The irony was that, no matter

> *The character and humour added by the director and team of animators is incredible. What started as a monologue becomes a mosaic of the absurd.'*
> **James Mather**

> *'Golly and I put together a short pilot to sell the idea, and to address the logistics of a series of this scale.'*
> **James Mather**

158

how hard we tried to prompt an interviewee, the best material was utterly unpredictable.'

After the initial three months of dialogue editing, and once the bulk of material had been completed, James moved on to other projects for a while before returning in order to garnish the completed episodes with sound effects. One of the great pleasures for James is seeing what has become of the interviews on which he started off working.

'The character and humour added by the director and team of animators is incredible,' he continues. 'What started as a monologue becomes a mosaic of the absurd, with touches of incidental action which exaggerate the stupidity of the situation. In order not to distract from the dialogue we carefully build up the atmosphere to create a realistic setting.'

Many of the atmospheres are specifically recorded for the series: waiting rooms, pet shops, aquariums and street activity, for example. On the other hand, the occasional car passing by, wing flaps or pig grunts come from a sound effects technician known as a foley artist, who sits in a room watching the film and creates sounds to coincide with the actions on screen – sometimes working live, in order to get the timing correct (although there's always the chance to go back and do it again) but more often inserting sounds from special CD compilations. How James and his crew decide what kinds of effects to use, and where to put them, depends hugely on the action created by the animator.

'Quite often there is more than one character in a shot,' he points out, 'although only one is usually talking. This allows us to have fun with the peripheral action, being careful not to be too distracting of course. Quite often Golly will reign in our suggestions, which can verge on scene stealing.'

Having spent so much time working on 'normal sounds', James was relieved that at least one of the episodes allowed him to be a little more creative…

'The addition of "Aliens" to the titles gave us the license to have a bit more fun with sound design,' he laughs: 'something we were limited on with the less surreal programmes.' He considers for a moment. 'Mind you,' he adds, 'a bunch of talking animals is hardly normal, is it?'

"There's only a certain depth you can go to, isn't there, without your head exploding."
Fergal the Shark

itle sequences and theme tunes have to encapsulate, within a few seconds, what a programme's all about, and prepare the audience for what they are about to see. Sometimes they are designed to be remembered and hummed for days afterwards, sometimes they are designed to be atmospheric but instantly forgettable, but they are always the hook keeping viewers right there in front of the screen.

Rory McLeod, the composer of *Creature Comforts'* instantly hummable theme, is a newcomer to film and TV work, but an old hand at live performance.

'I make songs,' he explains. 'I sing stories about my own life and my family, songs about my grandma… it's a kind of oral history, to keep the memories alive.'

Rory's musical style is eclectic, borrowing from traditions as widespread as Celtic folk tunes and African rhythms. Perhaps it has something to do with his background – his father hails from Glasgow and his mother's side of the family were Russian immigrants. Or perhaps it has more to do with his extensive travelling. Having worked with a Mexican circus for a while as a musical clown and fire-eater, he then spent time in Texas playing harmonica with a Reggae band. He has also scoured the globe for musical inspiration, from Asia, through the Middle East, Gambia, Cuba, Central America, Europe and Australia, to Africa.

The theme for *Creature Comforts* is the first piece of work Rory has had commissioned for television or film, but he has provided music for the stage before.

> **'I sing stories about my own life and my family, songs about my grandma… it's a kind of oral history, to keep the memories alive.'**
> **Rory McLeod**

'I did work with a theatre group in Scotland,' he says. 'We did a show based on Punch and Judy, and I wrote songs and music for that – creating moods and tension. As a songwriter that's what I do – I take people on a journey.'

The search for a musician to write the music for *Creature Comforts* took a long time, and involved a few false starts along the way. Golly eventually settled on Rory after he'd heard some of his songs, as Rory explains. 'Golly had heard my CDs before – I think he'd also seen me play. There was a calypso kind of song I made up about a girl I went to school with, and he liked the melody and the rhythm of that, so he asked for something in that style.'

However, the commission came at an inconvenient time for Rory.

'I was waiting for my wife to have a baby, up in the Orkneys, and I didn't have many instruments with me so I had to go and borrow some. I've used my harmonica as the main instrument, and I also have a trombone. My father-in-law has a mandolin so I borrowed that and learned to play it a bit. I used my mother-in-law's saucepans as a bit of colour. I used my foot, as well. I tied a spoon to my foot and tapped it on a box, and that gave me a bass drum kind of feel… But I did finally get the thing to them in time.'

Fortunately, Golly's requirements and Rory's style were perfectly matched. 'He wanted something lively and warm,' says Rory, 'and, looking at the samples of animation they sent me, I thought they were very earthy and human, so I was trying to make something that was accessible – not too polished, but with a lot of life. So I used acoustic instruments – I don't use samples or keyboards. There's quite a few changes in rhythm and accent in there, and I added some colour with the saucepans, so it's quite comic. It's quite dance-y.'

Given the constraints of television, it wasn't just a case of 'write us a theme tune' – the opening and closing credits had already been put together, and the music had to be exactly the right length. Fortunately, Rory regarded it as a challenge rather than a problem. 'They wanted an 18 second piece,' he recalls, 'and they wanted a piece lasting one minute and fifteen seconds, and they wanted a percussive piece for transitional use that had to be a minimum of forty five seconds. It was interesting to compress things into that small an amount of time.'

From beginning to end, it took Rory about three weeks to compose and record the theme for *Creature Comforts* – not including the time it took to learn the mandolin. Looking back on it now, he's very happy with the final result.

'I've never written music for film before,' he says, 'and it's an honour to create something for a series that I find quite poignant and entertaining.'

Rory McLeod.

'*I used my mother-in-law's saucepans as a bit of colour. I used my foot, as well. I tied a spoon to my foot and tapped it on a box…*'

Rory McLeod

publicity & marketing

Search for the phrase Creature Comforts on EBay – the internet auction site – and you'll usually find a large number of items of merchandise for sale. Besides the videos and DVDs there are cuddly toys (known as 'plush'), postcards, key-rings and ceramic figures… but mainly cuddly toys.

None of these items have anything to do with the new *Creature Comforts* series. They're all a legacy from the original short film, which means that they're now about fifteen years old. For TV or film merchandise to survive for that long is unusual. They are certainly still collectable.

When Nick Park made the original *Creature Comforts* there was no thought of merchandise. All that came later with the TV commercials. With the new series, and the benefit of hind-sight, Aardman has made a deliberate decision to get involved with the merchandizing right from the start. Partly this is a mechanism for increasing income (and remember, this *Creature Comforts* is costing far more to make than the original one did), and partly a way of raising public awareness. After all, the original film was shown on television with hardly any publicity, and only became popular through word of mouth. This one will arrive in a blaze of publicity.

'We were involved at some level right from the start because we had to sell the opportunity to licensees, therefore we had to familiarise ourselves with the property,' says Rachael Carpenter, Aardman's design and product development manager. 'The first things we saw were the animatics (rough videos cut together using the design sketches and the recorded voices) and the storyboards, because we had to start thinking early on about which potential partners we wanted to approach.'

One of the first decisions to involve Marketing was crucial – what should the new series be called? 'Ages ago there were some thoughts about whether we should still call it *Creature Comforts.* We did some focus tests and found that every-body knew *Creature Comforts*, but irritatingly they thought that the Heat Electric adverts were *Creature Comforts*.'

> "I hate seafood, I really absolutely detest it. I did eat a fish, once…"
> **Sapphire the Dolphin**

163

Image courtesy of Gosh

'There's already some awareness present — we're not trying to sell something that's completely unknown.'
Rachael Carpenter

The fact that people remembered the adverts more than the short film that spawned them has been a constant issue for Aardman from the early 1990s until now, but it actually helped Rachael and her colleagues to sell the merchandising to the new licensees.

'They recalled the characters, and remembered them as being funny,' she recalls. 'That has helped because there's already some awareness present – we're not going in and trying to sell something that's less well known as we had to do with *Angry Kid*, *Rex the Runt*, and, to some extent, *Chicken Run*. Everybody that we showed the clips of the new series to found it hysterical. You'd be sitting in the office, and in the meeting room someone would be presenting to a licensee, and you'd hear them laughing. It's never been a difficult job selling *Creature Comforts* to licensees.'

Lucy Wendover is part of the licensing and marketing team. One of her main jobs was to schedule the publicity and ensure that the right information was released at the right time. 'We did a press release about the time when we got the commission,' she says, 'but after that it's really been a question of making sure that we're keeping the profile high so that we can get our promotional partners on board. We're not trying to flood the market – we are going in very softly, building up demand and then, hopefully, doing a little bit more in 2004. Basically it's our job, with all our partners, to make *Creature Comforts* into as big an event as possible. Because it's a series of thirteen, ten-minute shorts that's going to go out on prime time ITV1, there's quite a lot of competition. But being animation it stands out and we have to make the most of that.'

Aardman's last major marketing experience had been with the movie *Chicken Run*, but there's a distinct difference between marketing a film and a TV series. Lucy explains, 'A feature film is current for about three months, then that's it. There's a massive marketing spend and then the bubble bursts and it's all over. But we know that *Creature Comforts* will be

Above: Trixie, transformed into a plush model. Below: The original Trixie model. Opposite: The Christmas episode should provide some useful material for cards.

enduring because of what it is.'

Whereas other film and TV companies often let the marketing opportunities influence events in the film – to the extent of sometimes including a character on the basis that it would make a cool toy – Aardman have always resisted this approach. 'We wouldn't create a series, or include anything in it, in the hope that we could then sell a load of products,' Lucy protests.

She adds, 'While marketing is very important to us, it is not at the forefront of production's mind. They're very focused on the animation. They don't want to compromise the integrity of the characters for the sake of a pair of slippers. How it translates into plush is not really important to them, so long as we do a good job.'

Above: A cuddly Captain Cuddlepuss. Below: The Captain as he appears in the series.

She adds, 'We have regular meetings with production, and tell them what we're doing and they help us. For example, they'll help us put the characters in the right pose for taking publicity shots, and they like our feedback when we tell them what our partners have said about the various edits. But we don't provide any input. We don't suggest it would be really good if the hamster could say, "Happy birthday, mum!" or anything like that. The marketing and the creative processes are entirely separate. We never interfere.'

'Another part of our job,' Lucy adds, 'is trying to build up the individual character profiles, which often means getting production to give us any extra information. We try and build the characters into personalities for people to engage with so that they'll start naming their pets after them.'

But that extra character information is not present in the interview transcripts or in the animations. 'Golly is quite resistant to all that,' Lucy sighs. 'He doesn't want us to assume anything extra about the characters. The only things that the creators can ever say are what has been said in the series. That's frustrating for us because people want to know more about what the characters are like. Take the hamster, for example. If you look at his set, and his environment, he's a forgotten pet, he has become part of the furniture. Why is that? The pizza that's in front of him, when was that eaten? How long ago? In other words, we've got to maximize interest without ruining the mystery.'

By now, things are moving at a fast pace. When the first episode of

'We don't suggest it would be really good if the hamster could say, "Happy birthday, mum!"'
Lucy Wendover

Creature Comforts is screened the production lines will have been running for weeks, if not months, creating replicas of the creatures in all kinds of forms. 'We are working on calendars, stationery, T-shirts, socks, mugs, key rings, all sorts of things,' Rachael says, 'but they will have a staggered release as we want to create a demand for the product. For the launch we're concentrating on the plush and stationery.'

But despite the merchandising, Rachael and Lucy are keen to emphasize the primacy of the TV episodes over everything else. 'The animation is always central to what we do,' Lucy says. 'That's what we want the consumers' first experience to be, so we try as much as possible to incorporate moving images or photography into the goods to show them the real thing. And the goods include books, DVD, and interactive cards with a chip inside so that you hear a voice when you open them up.'

As well as the obvious product tie-ins with greetings cards, soft toys, breakfast cereals, and so on, the marketing team at Aardman is also looking further afield. 'There are some really good pet food companies out there which are trying to find a slightly innovative approach to advertising,' Lucy says. 'To do something funny with a pet food company would be great. And pet insurance is a massive market. And then obviously I would love to have one of the animal charities on board, so long as the publicity keeps its humour and irony and does not take itself too seriously. And you can see the merchandise appearing in gardening shops with some of these characters.'

Plain sailing? Not always. Some difficult decisions have to be made about which characters to focus on. In the past the licensees were lucky because they already knew, for instance, that Frank the Tortoise was a hit with viewers. But given the large number of creatures being built for the new series, which ones are likely to get all the attention?

'From a marketing perspective, you have to focus on just a few characters because people won't remember more than a certain number,' Lucy explains. 'So we've based our decision on gut feeling and on people's reactions, the people who have watched it with us. We've also been influenced by the number of times that a character appears, which means that the cat and the dog (Captain Cuddlepuss and Trixie) are virtually spokespeople for the series.'

'They seem to encapsulate the whole essence of *Creature Comforts*,' Rachael agrees. 'They're sat on their sofa with a cup of tea, and they come up with some really funny one-liners. The slugs are brilliant as well, and they're a good example of characters who you wouldn't imagine being traditionally cute, translating into a product – cuddly soft toy slugs.'

Above and opposite: Aardman issues a style guide to licensees – including the publishers of this book – containing examples of merchandise showing suggested ways of using their artwork.

'On Chicken Run we were approached by a licensee who wanted to make processed chicken nuggets...'
Rachael Carpenter

Gary and Nigel are two gardening professionals who have worked their magic on the vegetable plots in the Portishead area. Nigel is a fan of organic gardening, as it means more peelings on the compost heap, and Gary's favourite shrub is called the Burning Bush.

Nigel is a very practical, unimaginative slug, whereas Gary is a bit more open to new concepts and ideas. In discussions on alien life, for instance, Nigel has repeatedly refused to speculate on what aliens might look like, whereas Gary is happy to give it a try.

Nigel can eat almost anything except for lychees and Turkish Delight, but he does have a problem with his weight. He is miffed that while his wife, Desiree, can lose weight without trying, he has to go on a strict regime of salad and fruit if he wants to shed a few pounds. Oddly for a slug, he quite likes salt.

One thing Gary and Nigel agree on is the value of dirt — always useful for a gardener. They both believe that you eat a pound of dirt in your lifetime without even knowing, and that dirt contains trace elements which builds up your resistance to infections. Who knows — they might be right.

"I reckon they've been on some sort of wacky backy-type stuff... if they're saying they've been abducted..."

'And then you have the emerging characters,' Lucy adds, 'like the hamster and the ones that appear in a lot of the episodes who have got a lot to say on lots of different subjects. We also focus on them. Mind you, Matilda the Performing Cow is an exception. She only appears in the *Circus* episode, I think, but she's so funny and the line she says about the raspberry is great.'

There are, of course, limits. Some characters, no matter how funny they might sound, are unlikely to translate into plush. 'Cuddly plankton?' Lucy wonders, 'I'm not sure about that!' And there are some items that just wouldn't be licensed, whatever happens. Aardman has strict rules about associating its characters with alcohol or cigarettes, given their animations' popularity amongst young audiences, but that doesn't stop some manufacturers from suggesting it. Then there are those proposals that are just so inappropriate that they boggle the mind. Rachael recalls, 'On *Chicken Run* we were approached by a licensee who wanted to make processed chicken nuggets, and that just wouldn't be appropriate!'

The animated films that Aardman has produced so far are popular right around the world, and the marketing plan has to assume that *Creature Comforts* will be no different although it is, perhaps, not as obviously international as, say, *Chicken Run*. Lucy explains, 'Japan should be a very keen market, and we are currently

"I'm quite low down in the food chain."
Ben the Shrimp

'*The licensees will produce a sample for a meeting and I'll say, "His eyes aren't right," or "His ears need moving."*'
Rachael Carpenter

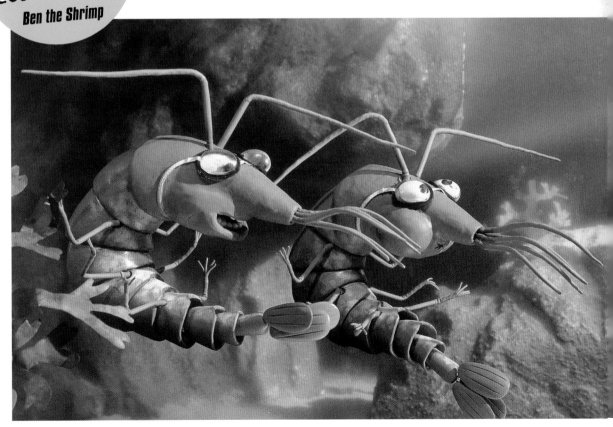

talking to people in the US. The difficulty is, obviously, that this is a very British series reflecting the attitudes of the British and even the animals are sort of British animals. And remember that in the States, eight-minute programmes don't work particularly well, you really need a minimum of twenty-two minutes. But we hope that it will travel as well as the original *Creature Comforts*.'

The licensing and marketing team does not just brief potential licensees and negotiate the terms under which the characters will be used because nothing is allowed to go into production, unless it has been seen and approved by the marketing team. 'Absolutely everything comes in for approval at every stage,' Rachael confirms. 'We see things at concept, then the finished artwork, and the prototypes. We're working on plush at the moment and, taking the cat as an example, the licensees will produce a sample for a meeting and I'll say, "His eyes aren't right," or "His ears need moving," and then it'll to go back to the Far East and get re-made. And they'll keep presenting it until I am completely satisfied. Once we reach that stage the cat can go into production.'

But when creating the merchandise there can be problems. For example, the model as seen on TV is not complete. It does not need to

"I think I would really like to just be groomed occasionally, during my tea breaks."
Vivian the Crab

'We've got to maximize interest without ruining the mystery.'
Lucy Wendover

be because only its front is filmed, and the worm, for instance, only has its top half seen. So what should the back of the cat or the lower half of the worm look like on the toy merchandising? That's where a little creative interpretation is needed to turn them into 3-dimensional characters.

But, despite all the hard work by the Aardman team in selecting the licensees and working with them, it has not always been easy. Rachael explains, 'Frank the Tortoise has been very hard for the licensees to get right. When they first presented him I nearly cried because he needed so much work. However they have done a great job and he's now looking good.'

Sadly, Frank doesn't feature as much in the new series as in the last. For various reasons he has been slightly eclipsed by other characters. This can cause some tension with the client companies, as Lucy explains. 'They'll all be saying "I want Frank" and we'll be saying, "But what about the other characters?" I don't know how we're going to do it, but we have to think how we're going to juggle the Frank-but-no-Frank problem.'

Frank comes out of his shell for the camera.

Hopefully, less of a problem will be the chance to create follow-up adverts just as the original *Creature Comforts* gave rise to the Heat Electric adverts. 'We would really like to have a partner, if the scripts and the brand are right,' Lucy says, 'because it's very good to keep *Creature Comforts* alive and out there. We'd either use existing characters – if the product really suited the cat and the dog we'd re-interview them – or create new ones.'

'New animation might also be required for the ITV "idents,"' Lucy explains, referring to the short, specially filmed items that lead into the ITV programmes, 'where you have a celebrity backstage with the camera panning around them. They want to do that for *Creature Comforts*, and it'd be great if we can pull it off, but how do you do it? The characters don't go backstage. They don't have a backstage! If ITV can find the budget for us, it would mean new animation. But right at the moment I'd say it's very tricky.'

In conclusion, it's fair to say that while most of the creative team working on *Creature Comforts* are focussing on individual decisions and small areas of work, the marketing and publicity personnel are covering a huge number of highly important decisions. They are a vitally important piece of the jigsaw, and the work is no less creative than, say, designing a character or building a set. And, like those more traditional Aardman skills, the job comes down to the same, simple core value. As Lucy Wendover says, 'We always try to put plenty of thought and imagination into what we do.'

'I don't know how we're going to do it, but we have to think how we're going to juggle the Frank-but-no-Frank problem.'
Lucy Wendover

172

missing characters & lost episodes

One of the things that the *Creature Comforts* team very quickly discovered was that it often got more than it bargained for during the interviews. Faced with a sympathetic questioner, some interviewees opened up completely giving not only their opinions on all kinds of subjects but also their personal histories, insights into their home lives and their secret thoughts and feelings. Some material had to be rejected, while other material was considered very carefully before being used. After all, even though the words were being put into the mouths of small model animals, the voices were still those of real people who might be recognized by their friends.

'People inevitably give away more than they realize,' Golly confirms. 'People do because they soon forget that the tape recorder is there. One interviewee in particular did give rise to some concerns. He talked frankly in a strong Norfolk accent about his medical history and his numerous run-ins with doctors in various hospitals and surgeries, and his words were brought to life by a doleful bloodhound. He's one of the funniest characters in the entire series, but the worry was that he might take exception to being portrayed in that way. And that he'd realize he'd said too much. So we contacted him and found that he was very happy to be in the show, and kept him in.'

However, some creatures that seemed like good ideas at the time were not kept in, not because the interviewees were giving away too much about themselves, but because there was something indefinably wrong about the combination of voice and animal. 'There was one character that I really liked, a Canadian Beagle,' says Toby Farrow, who recorded some of the interviews and transcribed others, and safeguards all the interview material. 'He was quite acidic, very... bitter is the wrong word, but he had a very dry outlook on life. I thought he was fantastic, but he sounded a bit vicious somehow.'

'It would be nice, maybe on DVD, to do a slightly X-rated version...'
Gareth Owen

Seamus Malone working with early small models of Trixie and Captain Cuddlepuss. These models were later scaled up, along with the sofa and set, in order to speed up animation.

Another production change involved the Christmas episode, which was originally to have featured Mrs Santa and a factory full of elves. A late decision to remove them was the result of concerns over mixing the overtly fantastic into the comfy *Creature Comforts* mix.

Possibly the biggest regret that the team have is the loss of an entire episode early in the production process. Most of the themes for the episodes are pretty innocuous – *Pets at the Vets*, *The Circus*, and *Christmas Comforts* – but there was one that might have raised a few hackles if it had ever been screened.

'Yeah, there's a whole episode that was planned and lost along the way,' admits production manager Gareth Owen. 'It was called *Lab. Animals*, which is a bit close to the bone. It was about people's attitudes to laboratory animals – some of them have strong attitudes, but a lot of people are fairly indifferent or don't know the reality and are not prepared to put themselves on the line, so it never really worked. And from my point of view, I've got a lot of friends who wouldn't have liked it.'

An out-take sequence in which Trixie is crushed by a falling tin of Spam.

Golly agrees. 'I wanted to do an episode on laboratory animals in a very Gary Larson way,' he says, referring to the American cartoonist best known for his *Far Side* series. 'But in fact we found it just didn't work. We had a smoking beagle, and two dogs pinned to a board covered in electrodes all complaining about animal testing and how unfair it was. It's funny out of context, but as soon as you make an episode it just becomes very miserable and depressing.'

'I thought it was very poignant,' Toby Farrow adds, 'because you've got animals in this awful situation and they're either unaware of it, or railing against it. We worked on it for a long time and were very careful to make it clear that the animals weren't passive, that they were angry about their position or simply unknowing about what was to happen. For example, we had a pig innocently saying, "I'm sure animals don't mind being cut up…" It's the dramatic irony – he doesn't realize what his fate is going to be, which is what makes it funny.'

Lucy Wendover, of the Aardman publicity and marketing team, would have had to sell the idea of a rather disturbing *Lab. Animals*

'There's a whole episode that was planned and lost along the way…'
Gareth Owen

episode, and she wasn't particularly looking forward to the idea. As she explains, 'The companies looking to put *Creature Comforts* images onto greetings cards and soft toys were uneasy about the idea. From the marketing and publicity point of view, we were open to it, but the decision to drop the idea eventually came from production. They're making a series for a family audience, and if one of those episodes sits outside that remit then it's a problem.'

> **'People inevitably give away more than they realize... because they soon forget that the tape recorder is there.'**
>
> **Golly**

In the end, it was decided that the early evening slot, along with the light-hearted nature of the rest of the episodes, meant that *Lab. Animals* was a non-starter. It would have stuck out like a sore thumb and upset a lot of people, especially small children who might have been watching. And yet, in the minds of some of the Aardman team, there's still a little bit of yearning for that which they lost. And, perhaps, a desire to use some of the material they can never show on terrestrial television.

'It would be nice,' Toby Farrow says, 'maybe on DVD, to do a slightly X-rated version...'

An elderly alien in a tartan wrap is questioned under strong lights. The design was later changed.

looking to the future

From Richard Goleszowski's office you can clearly see out into the large workshop where the models for *Creature Comforts* are being built. On two long, battered, knife-scarred and Plasticine-splattered wooden benches, a row of brightly coloured donkeys, rats, pigs and the like are in various stages of construction, being held up by metallic clamps for all the world like specimens ready for dissection in a biology class. Model makers carefully work on them, scraping away a bit of excess Plasticine here, adding a bit more detail there, until they are finished but not too perfect, as Golly continually reminds them. And around the walls are pinned the original sketches of the characters, drawn by Golly, Nick Park and Michael Salter. Some of the sketches are of animals that were never, in the end, made. Other sketches have lists of possible character names attached to them, as the people who pass through the workshop make their various suggestions.

"Dirt on food, dirt on food, what, what, dirt on food can kill you."
Anthony the Pig

Across the other side of the workshop is the office where the sound editing is being done. The door is usually wide open, and from the doorway drift random words, repeated time after time until they lose all meaning, and giggles looping endlessly around and around while the editor seeks just the right moment to cut them.

There's a rack just outside the workshop on which the completed models lie, wrapped in transparent plastic, their eyes barely visible as they stare into nothing. Some of them have had their brief exposure to fame; others are still waiting for their moment. Eventually they will all be packed into boxes and stored away, being brought out for exhibitions and special occasions.

Just around the corner, the cavernous studio space has been partitioned off into dozens of cubicles. Inside some of them, small recreations of suburban life are being bolted, nailed and screwed together. Inside others, similar sets are being taken apart again, and the pieces meticulously stored away or recycled for other sets. And one or two of

the cubicles have curtains covering the doorways, and signs set at eye level instructing people not to enter because animation is in progress.

There's a good feeling, spreading right across the Aardman building where *Creature Comforts* is being assembled. It's a feeling made up of a mixture of excitement and comfort, and it's shared by a group of people who feel as if they've caught their first sight of something familiar after a long journey. For some of them this *is* something very familiar, for they worked on the original *Creature Comforts*, fourteen years ago now. For others it's a new feeling because they only saw it on television, and possibly joined Aardman because of that. But they all feel proud to be a part of this.

And will there be a next time? Another series? Nothing formal has been announced, but the production team are already whispering about the possibility. Initial thoughts are that the theme might spring out of the *Aliens* episode of the second series, with interviews being conducted abroad trying to get a foreign perspective on what it means to be British (and, perhaps, *vice-versa*). And after that? Well, that depends on the audience figures, but there's always the possibility that more episodes could be made. If nothing else, it's a training ground for new animators and, given the amount of work they do, Aardman will always need plenty of them...

Below: Stan and Ted, the baby birds.

"Cat papoo and dog papoo ... and bird papoo."

Stan

Part Four:
Last Things Last

conclusion

I t's not that often you see someone who is professional and keen at the same time. The two words don't normally go together. Professional and blasé – yes, they go together nicely. Film sets and television studios are full of people who display both qualities in abundance. Keen and amateur, they go together too. But professional and keen? That's like asking for a dessert that's rich, creamy *and* low fat.

Perhaps that's one of the reasons why the atmosphere at Aardman is so unusual and so invigorating. There's no doubting the professionalism of the staff – it's obvious in every second of animated material they produce. But what's also obvious is that they still get passionate about what they do. They enjoy being there. It's hard work with long hours, but they feel that they are part of something worthwhile, and they're making their own measurable contributions.

A lot of this feeling has to do with the ethos of the company. Peter Lord and David Sproxton have, despite the passage of more than twenty years and the kind of international success that would make many larger companies jealous, managed to make Aardman feel like a small outfit operating out of someone's shed (and that's a good thing, by the way). Any organization where the people at the top are on first name terms with the people at the bottom has to be respected.

Despite Aardman's major international success, they haven't forgotten their roots. They know that, despite *Chicken Run*, people still remember them for Morph, Wallace and Gromit, and *Creature Comforts*. The pressure on them to produce more and more material to cash in on that success would be enough to squash some people like Plasticine, but they've held firm. Rather than churn out a new Wallace and Gromit movie every Christmas, for instance, they've moved cautiously, only going ahead when they were sure that they had something new and interesting to say, when they were sure that they could better their last attempt. And the fact that it's taken them fourteen years to return to *Creature Comforts* – the series that won them their first BAFTA award and their first Oscar® – says a lot about their own restraint and the respect in which they hold their audience. If this were any other company, people would be talking about the *Creature Comforts* franchise. Here, at Aardman, it's not a franchise, it's a work of art.

Binky the dog, looking eager.

It's hard, when you're producing four seconds of material per day, to maintain the vision of what the finished series will look like.

The new *Creature Comforts* is, of course, on a totally different scale from the first *Creature Comforts*. It's not only about fifteen times as long, requiring many times the number of people to make it, but it comes with a fully fledged marketing campaign in place, licenses for the spin-off products already signed, and the special features for the DVD release in hand.

One needs to keep reminding oneself that the new *Creature Comforts* is, in total, longer than some movies but it feels small scale and intimate, which says something for the skills of director Golly and his team at structuring the episodes and coming up with the various themes. It also says something about the skills of the animators. It's hard, when you're producing four seconds of material per day, to maintain the vision of what the finished series will look like. It's all too easy to get fixated on the movement of an arm, the waggle of some fingers or the way an ear twitches. And yet, talking to the animators, one knows that they all understand the overall scheme, and the part they play in it.

Three things have remained constant across the years separating the original *Creature Comforts* from the new one, and these things will guarantee its success.

First is the actual look of the episodes. Television has developed in a major way in the intervening years. Today's shows would have been regarded as chaotic and frenetic then, what with the current weakness of TV directors for rapid editing, tilted angles and sudden cuts to black and white or grainy, *cinema vérité* footage. And shows that were then regarded as cutting edge would now be considered slow and overly struc- tured. But the new *Creature Comforts*

Mr Tickles, the performing seal – an expert at tootling the horn.

Chappy ruminates at Sunny Villa Farm.

goes on, as normal. And that's despite the fact that the construction of the models and the way they are filmed has changed. The team has managed to make the new series look like the old, as if the original could be shown again without anyone noticing much difference. Partly that's a result of Golly's repeated insistence that he doesn't care if there are thumbprints on the models, but partly it's due to the fact that stop-motion animation itself reached its peak in the 1950s, and hasn't really developed since then. It still looks the same.

Second is the continuity of the team working on the show. Golly was employed by Aardman when the original *Creature Comforts* was made, and he's directing the new one. Andy MacCormack was a film cameraman on the original *Creature Comforts* and is now director of photography. Other members of the team have worked on both versions, including Julie Lockhart. And Nick Park is there, ensuring that the vision he had all those years ago is replicated faithfully in the twenty-first century.

And third, and possibly most importantly, is the universal appeal of the show. Listening to the animals talking is like listening to ourselves. As we hear their opinions, their squabbles, their troubles, we can't help but wonder what kind of animal *we* might have made – and that of course is the enduring appeal of *Creature Comforts*.

by Pickles the Guide Dog

I like to be helpful, I really do, it's what I think my life's all about, really. Helping people. If someone's in trouble, or they need a favour, then I'd like to think I'm the first person to step forward and help. So when they asked me to write a few words to go at the end of this book I jumped at the chance, of course I did.

The only problem is that I can't really remember who it was who asked me. I can remember the face as clear as I can remember my own – not that you remember your own face, but you see it often enough in mirrors and shop windows as you're passing by, don't you? But I can't remember the name. Isn't that odd?

I do remember being interviewed. I remember that distinctly. A rather nice man asked me some rather odd questions. Toby, yes, that's it. The name. I think. He reminded me of our caretaker. I once chased him through the car park with some mistletoe in my hand, but he was too fast for me. Anyway, this young man, Toby, was asking me about unidenti-flying objects, and do I believe in life on other planets or wher-ever. I told him firmly that God only makes things perfect, and these alien things aren't perfect are they? They're all green and slimy when you see them on the TV. So they don't exist.

Whoever it was who asked me to write some words at the end of this book asked me to say something about what the book is like. The best thing I can think of to say is that it's a bit like spam. I think spam's a mixture of, umm, intestines of animals and stuff like that. It's bits of animals that aren't very appealing, like a sheep's eyeball or the intes-tine of a cow or something like that, and they mix it all up in a mixer and then they call it spam. Well this book's a bit like that. It's lots of different things, like interviews, and photographs, and things that we've all said, and stuff I don't really understand about Plasticine and lights and things, all mixed up together. You see what I mean? I'm not saying it's lots of unappealing things all mixed together, although it's not to my taste I'm afraid. I'm just saying that there's a lot in the book.

I'm afraid I can't write any more because I've got a lot to do, but I hope that you enjoyed reading the book, and I hope that you enjoyed seeing us all on TV. I don't have a TV – wicked things – but I'm sure someone will tell me what it was like. And I hope that the young man comes back to ask me some more questions, although I do think he should be concentrating more on matters of the spirit. That would make a much more interesting programme than all this stuff about clowns, and aliens, and beaches.

Series created by Nick Park

Featuring the voices of the Great British Public

Associate Producer	Abbie Ross
Production Manager	Gareth Owen
Production Co-ordinator	Helen Argo
Pre-Production	Cindy Jones
	Bridget Mazzey
Floor Manager	Richard 'Beeky' Beek
Floor Assistant	Dean Ferris

Script Editor	Toby Farrow
Interviewers	Karen Bidewell, Mindell Bowen, Steve Cole, Andrew Carter, Jane Devoy, Kim Lenaghan, Wendy Rickard, Graeme Rose, Kate Towsey, Zbigniew Trzaska, Gerald Tyler and Rob Young

Sound Recordists	Toby Hughes and Mark Swinglehurst
Key Transcriber	Susan Fry

Character Design	Michael Salter
Additional Character Design	Sylvie Bennion, Nigel Davies
Head of Model-making	Kate Anderson
Model Makers	Arlene Arrell, Chris Brock, Claire Drewitt, Amanda Darby, Cath Ford, Ben Greenwood, Mick Hockney, Rob Horvath, Neil Jones, Virginia Mason, Debbie Smith, Harriet Thomas and James Young

Art Director	Kitty Clay
Set Build	Cliff Thorne Scenic Construction
Senior Prop Maker	Jane Kite
Props and Sets	Justeen Bailey, Claire Baker, Andy Brown, Duncan Miller, Rachel Moore, Bridget Phelan, Manon Roberts and Kathryn Williams

Animators	Phil Beglan, Claire Billet, Terry Brain, Darren Burgess, Dug Calder, Miki Cash, Stefano Cassini, Merlin Crossingham, Jo Fenton, Jay Grace, Suzy Parr, Pascual Perez, Dan Ramsey, Chris Sadler, Andy Symanowski, Darren Thompson, Ian Whitlock and Lee Wilton
Additional Animation	Peter Peake and Rich Webber

Computer Animation	Stefan Marjoram
Additional Computer Animation	Dave Bennett
Assistant Animators	Alison Evans, Maria Hopkinson-Hassell,
	Jack Slade and Andy Spilsted
Directors of Photography	Andy MacCormack
	Frank Passingham
Lighting Camera	Toby Howell
Additional Lighting Camera	Charles Copping
Camera Assistant	Churton Season
Gaffers	Richard Hosken, Clive Scott
Rigger	Alan 'Scratch' Scrase
Sound Design	Soundbyte Studios
Supervising Sound Editor	James Mather
Assistant Sound Editor	Joseph Stracey
Mix	Wounded Buffalo
Foley	Paul Ackerman
Editors	Will Ennals
	Andrew Hassenruck
	Dan Lincoln
	Dave MacCormick
Editorial Assistant	Stuart Bruce
Voice Breakdown	Helen Garrard and Nick Upton
Visual FX	Mike Shirra
Post Production	The Pink House
Music	Rory McLeod
Titles	Olly Reid at Hothead Films
Executive Producers	Peter Lord, David Sproxton, Nick Park, Liz Keynes
Producer	Julie Lockhart
Director	Richard Goleszowski
For Aardman:	
Image Bank Administrator	Sharron Traer
Design Executive	Kate Strudwick
Design and Product Development Manager	Rachael Carpenter
Licensing Manager	Helen Dunkley

index

acknowledgements

Andy Lane would like to record his grateful thanks to:

Rachael Carpenter and Helen Argo, for setting up all the
    interviews so professionally;

Peter Lord, Nick Park, Kate Anderson, Rachael Carpenter, Kitty
    Clay, Toby Farrow, Richard 'Golly' Goleszowski, Jay Grace,
    Dan Lincoln, Julie Lockhart, Stefan Marjoram, James Mather,
    Andy MacCormack, Rory McLeod, Gareth Owen,
    Michael Salter and Lucy Wendover for explaining
    their craft to me so enthusiastically;

Helen Grimmett, for transcribing the interviews so accurately;

Dan Newman, for designing the book
    so brilliantly;

Andrew Martin, for obtaining the old
    interview material so diligently;

and Natalie Jerome, for editing the
    book so perceptively.

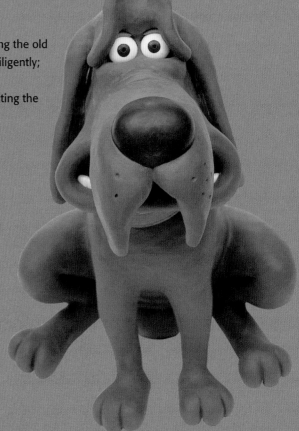

"Sorry, what was the question again?"
Clement

192